Margaret's Recipes

From Her Tea Rooms

by

Margaret Bacon

Photography Haydn Rogers
Design Brendan Rallison
Printing Broadgate Printers

First published in Great Britain in 2004 by
Margaret Bacon
Revised and reprinted 2004

Copyright © Margaret Bacon Author 2004
Copyright © Photography "Images by Haydn Rogers" 2004
Publishers: Margaret and Roger Bacon.

ISBN: 0-9547914-0-1

Design and Artwork by Brendan Rallison Ltd.

Photography by Images by Haydn Rogers.

Printed and bound in Great Britain
by Broadgate Printers, Aylsham.

CONTENTS

Introduction   9

Quick Conversion Guide   14

Morning Tea

How to make the perfect cup of tea   16

Plain Shortbread Biscuit   17

Florentines   18

Almond/Cherry Topped Shortbread   19

Chocolate Covered Fudge Fingers   21

Ginger Iced Shortbread   22

Nutty Flapjacks   23

Gingerbread People   25

Chocolate Orange Biscuit   27

Date, Apricot or Fig Slice   28

Plain Scones   29

Norfolk Honey Butter   30

Basic Plain Scone - *Electric Mixer*   30

Plain Scones - *Hand Method*   31

Norfolk Scone   33

Lemon/Sultana Scones   34

Spicy Fruit Scones   36

Banana and Hazelnut Scones   37

Stilton and Walnut Scones   38

Cheese/Herb Scones   40

Strawberry/Gooseberry Jam   41

Raspberry or Loganberry Jam   42

Blackcurrant/Rhubarb Jam   43

Apricot Jam   44

Pineapple Jam   45

Mag's English Muffins   47

Spicey Teacakes   48

Home-Made Mincemeat   49

Bread Basket

Basic Bread Recipe   53

Walnut, Pecan Nut or Brazil Nut Bread   54

Stilton, Apricot & Walnut Loaves   57

Cheese & Sun Dried Tomato Bread   58

Savoury Lunch

Mushroom and Pecan Nut Soup   60

Parsnip & Apple Soup   61

Cauliflower and Stilton Soup   62

Carrot & Orange Soup   63

Bacon & Egg Pie   64

Stilton, Apricot & Walnut Flan   65

Roast Vegetable & Cheese Flan   66

Cranberry, Chicken & Almond Flan   67

Smoked Salmon & Spinach Flan   69

Salmon & Cheese Flan   70

Desserts

Fig Custard Tart	72
Pecan Pie	73
Almond Bakewell Tart	74
Quick Almond Pudding	75
Fruit Pies	76
Shortcrust Pastry - *Hand Method*	77
Shortcrust Pastry - *Electric Mixer*	77
Mincemeat Galette	78
Brandy Butter	78
Almond Slice	80

Cakes and Sweets

Marmalade Bread Pudding	83
Sticky Date Cake	84
Pineapple Fruit Cake	84
Ginger Cake	86
Ginger Icing	86
Banana & Brazil Nut Loaf	87
Orange / Apricot Cake	89
Coffee & Walnut Cake	90
Coffee Butter Cream	90
Apricot & Coconut Cake	93
Lemon Pound Cake	94
Lemon Icing	94
Fruit Loaves	95
Lemon and Sultana Cake	97
Lemon Butter Cream	97
Fresh Cream Eclairs	98
Chocolate Glacé Icing	98
Fresh Cream Meringues	101
Chocolate Chip Squares	102
Victoria Sponge Cake	105
Basic Sponge Cake - *Electric Mixer*	106
Basic Sponge Cake - *Hand Method*	107
Small Buns and Butterfly Cakes	109
Glacé Icing	109
Butter Cream	109
Dundee Cake	110
Simnel Cake	110
Rich Fruit Cake	113
Marzipan	114
Royal Icing	114
Carrot & Walnut Cake	115
Toppings for Carrot Cake	116
Cream Cheese Frosting	
Rum Icing	
Orange Icing	
Quick & Easy Fruit Cake	117
Mince Pies	119
Brandy Snaps	121
Wyn's Christmas Pudding	122
Apple / Sultana Cake	124

INTRODUCTION

The year 2003 was for Roger and me the realisation of an eleven-year ambition to win the Top Tea Place of Great Britain Award.

We had already been running our first teashop in the Norfolk Broads area for five and a half years and hadn't actually heard of the Tea Council Award until we were invited to become a member of the Tea Council Guild. As a member of the Guild, our name automatically went forward as a contender.

We could never have imagined when we moved to this beautiful county of Norfolk, 32 years ago, on our Wedding Day, that we would encounter such lifestyle changes. We were living in Hemsby. Roger was a Woodwork Teacher in Great Yarmouth and I was a School Secretary. Time elapsed and Roger came to realise that actually his main love was for woodwork and not for teaching. He dreamed of becoming a self-employed Furniture Maker. He took the plunge and within a year or two, he was able to show his work at various exhibitions around the country. His orders steadily trickled in. I continued with my employment, spending most of my holidays helping to promote Roger's work.

After twelve years, we came to realise that we needed a permanent showroom. We found the perfect place in the centre of Ludham, a village in the Norfolk Broad's area. It was a lock-up shop with an outbuilding behind the shop, which had been previously used by a saddler and harness maker as a workshop.

The only way we could possibly afford to buy the shop was by selling our home. This we did and in doing so, made ourselves homeless.

With the help of friends, and eventually moving to live in the back of the shop, with all the luxury of an outside toilet and a tin bath, we were able to get the shop up and running.

Fortunately, Roger was able to rent a workshop in the village and in addition to Roger's furniture; we were able to sell the work of other craftspeople and artists.

We eventually obtained Planning Permission to convert the outbuilding behind the shop to living accommodation, thereby providing us with a uniquely designed one-bedroomed flat with a very small interconnecting kitchen.

At about this time I decided it was time to resign from my job to take full time control of the shop. I had never fully enjoyed working in offices and had always longed to do something more creative. My main hobbies had been cookery and needlework.

I decided to embark on a needlework course part time, which fitted in very well with the running of the shop.

A further three years elapsed. We were enjoying our time in Ludham but being a holiday area trade tended to be seasonal. I was sitting in the shop one day when it occurred to me that it might be possible to combine my favourite hobby of cooking with the craft shop. The one question I was constantly being asked was 'where can we get a cup of tea'. There wasn't a teashop in the village. Our shop was in the perfect setting and I loved baking. Space was a problem but after a lot of re-arrangement and all the relevant Council

permission, we re-opened as a craft/teashop on the 1st November 1987.

We had only two tables, covered with Nottingham lace tablecloths, eight chairs, two new kettles and china crockery.

From the outset I reasoned that everything we served in the teashop should be genuinely home-made.

Initially within my limitations, I just made cakes, scones and biscuits. Word spread and eventually two tables increased to four inside the shop. Later we added two in the tiny courtyard garden. I couldn't believe my eyes during the summer months when we experienced queues.

As time went by, we felt we needed more living space. I realised I had found my forté, so we decided after five and a half years of tea-making, we would expand. It was at this time we found Chestnut Farm House for sale in the tiny village of Baconsthorpe in North Norfolk. Nothing in the world could have persuaded us to leave Norfolk. The house was in a very rundown condition, but with Roger's former training in the woodwork trade, he felt confident in undertaking most of the projects. The property was able to provide us with enough potential to expand the tea-rooms, a workshop for Roger and the provision of our own car parking facilities.

Our third risk taking adventure was about to begin. We moved into the house on the 11th May 1992. We lived in one room whilst the builders completed the damp course and lots of repair work. The kitchen was kitted out and by the 1st August we were in business once again, serving teas in the first of the three downstairs reception rooms, which we called the

Harebell Parlour. Eventually we opened the Strawberry and Rose Parlours. The following summer we were able to serve teas in the garden as well.

We became so busy; Roger decided to help full-time in the tea-rooms and now makes the furniture in his precious limited spare time.

We now have 17 years experience of running a tea-room, during which time I have been able to expand my knowledge of cooking. Being self-taught, it is surprising how quickly one can learn when faced with the daily pressures of running a business. I regret never having had the opportunity of a formal training but I have been able to develop my own individual style and feel that there is no substitute for personal experience.

I feel proud that after all these years I am still able to produce all the food served in the tea-rooms. Over the years, we have received five Awards of Excellence from the Tea Council. We were voted the 2001 Norfolk Tea Room of the Year. I always said I would like to win the Top Tea Place Award once and if I ever did that would be the year I would produce a recipe book in order to share my secrets! 2003 is the year and here are the recipes.

I would like to take this opportunity to say a very big thank you to Roger who has supported me through every trial and tribulation over the years. He labours tirelessly in the background and without his love and support there would not be a 'Margarets'.

A special thank you goes to the staff I have employed over the past 17 years. Tea and food of course are a very important side of the business, but without loyal staff to serve our customers and run the establishment we could not operate. A special thank you goes to my first and longest standing member of staff Sylvia who supported me loyally for 12 years.

Last but by no means least; I would like to take this opportunity to thank all my customers for their support over the years.

QUICK CONVERSION GUIDE

(These conversions are approximate only)

DRY MEASURES

Metric	Imperial
15g	½oz
30g	1oz
60g	2oz
90g	3oz
125g	4oz (¼ lb)
155g	5oz
185g	6oz
220g	7oz
250g	8oz (½ lb)
280g	9oz
315g	10oz
345g	11oz
375g	12oz (¾ lb)
410g	13oz
440g	14oz
470g	15oz
500g	16oz (1 lb)
750g	24oz (1½ lb)
1kg	32oz (2 lb)

LIQUID MEASURES

30ml	1 fluid oz
60ml	2 fluid oz
100ml	3 fluid oz
125ml	4 fluid oz
150ml	5 fluid oz (¼ pint / 1 gill)
190ml	6 fluid oz
250ml	8 fluid oz
300ml	10 fluid oz (½ pint)
500ml	16 fluid oz
600ml	20 fluid oz (1 pint)
1000ml (1 litre)	1¾ pints

OVEN TEMPERATURE
(The oven temperatures are only a guide)

	°C (Celsius)	°F (Fahrenheit)	Gas Mark
Very slow	120	250	1
Slow	150	300	2
Moderately slow	160	325	3
Moderate	180-190	350-375	4
Moderately hot	200-210	400-425	5
Hot	220-230	450-475	6
Very hot	240-250	500-525	7

As you work your way through the recipes please don't be alarmed at the constant reference to the 'food processor'.

I have written all the recipes as I have become accustomed to making them for the tea-rooms. Of course all the recipes can be produced using traditional hand methods or by using an electric mixer.

14

Morning Tea

HOW TO MAKE THE PERFECT CUP OF TEA

Always use good quality loose leaf or bagged tea.

Always fill the kettle with freshly drawn cold water.

When brewing black and oolong teas, allow the water to reach boiling point before pouring onto the leaves.

When brewing green tea, boil the water and then allow it to cool slightly before pouring on to the leaves.

Measure the tea carefully into the pot. Use one tea bag or one rounded teaspoon of loose tea for each cup to be served.

Allow the tea to brew for the correct number of minutes.

Small leafed black tea normally needs 2-3 minutes.

Larger leafed black tea needs 3-5 minutes.

Oolong teas need 5-7 minutes.

Green teas need 1-3 minutes.

Where possible, follow instructions on packets or test each tea to find the number of minutes that suits.

Margaret's Recipes *From Her Tea Rooms*

PLAIN SHORTBREAD BISCUIT

Ingredients

375g – 12oz Plain Flour

250g – 8oz Butter

140g – 4½ oz Caster Sugar

6 Glacé cherries for decoration

Baking Tin
9" / 23cm diameter x 1" / 2.5 cm
deep (greased and lined)

Oven 180°C / 350° F / Gas Mark 4

Place all the ingredients in the food processor and mix until a soft ball is formed.

Press into the lined baking dish. Smooth and prick the shortbread with a fork.

Divide into 12 equal portions in the tin and place a half cherry in the centre of each.

Bake in the oven for approximately 35 minutes.

Leave in the tin to cool.

Sprinkle a little caster sugar on top to serve.

FLORENTINES

Ingredients

60g – 2oz Sultanas

60g – 2oz Mixed Fruit & Peel

90g – 3oz Cornflakes (crushed)

125g – 4oz Glacé Cherries –
chopped (mixed colours if possible)

90g – 3oz Slivered Almonds

405g Tin Condensed Milk

125g – 4oz Good Quality
Chocolate of your choice

Oven 160°C / 325°F / Gas Mark 3

Place the sultanas, mixed fruit & peel,
cherries, cornflakes, almonds and condensed
milk in a large bowl.

Mix until well combined.

Put spoons full of the mixture onto prepared
Bakewell paper, on a baking tray. Space
about two inches apart and bake in the oven
for approximately 25-30 minutes, until firm.

Allow to cool before coating one side with
the melted chocolate of your choice.

ALMOND/CHERRY TOPPED
SHORTBREAD

Ingredients

375g – 12oz Plain Flour

250g – 8oz Butter
(room temperature)

140g - 4½ oz Caster Sugar

50g - 2oz Flaked Almonds

1 Teaspoon Almond Extract

For Decoration

30g – 1oz Flaked Almonds

4 Glacé Cherries (halved)

*Baking Tin – 9" / 23cm x 1" /
2.5cm deep (greased and lined)
Oven 180°C / 350° / Gas Mark 4*

Place the flour, butter, caster sugar, almonds and almond extract in the food processor and mix until a soft ball is formed.

Press into the lined baking dish, smooth the top. Divide into 8 portions. Sprinkle over the top the remaining flaked almonds. Place half a cherry in the centre of each portion.

Cook in the centre of the oven for approximately 45-50 minutes.

Leave in the tin until cold.

Walnuts, Brazil nuts or hazel nuts are equally delicious in the recipe as an alternative to the almonds.

Nothing compares with the aroma of home baking.
I can resist most things but freshly cooked shortbread is very tempting indeed.

19

Chocolate Covered Fudge Fingers

Ingredients

250g – 8oz Butter

250g – 8oz Granulated Sugar

1 Tin Condensed Milk (405g)

2 Tablespoons Golden Syrup

500g – 1lb Biscuit Crumbs –
(preferably of a shortbread variety)

Good quality chocolate of
your choice for coating.

*Greased and lined baking tin -
10 1/2" / 26cm x 7" / 18cm*

Put the butter, sugar, condensed milk and golden syrup into a large microwaveable dish.

Cook on high for 7-8 minutes or until boiling point is reached. Stir the mixture carefully every 2-3 minutes.

Turn the setting to 'simmer' and continue cooking for a further 7-8 minutes.

In the meantime, crumb the biscuits by crushing them. Biscuits can also be crushed in a food processor.

Add the crumbs to the mixture and stir thoroughly. Quickly pour into the prepared lined baking tin, and smooth.

When cold, cover the top with melted chocolate of your choice and cut into finger shapes.

GINGER ICED SHORTBREAD

Ingredients

Shortbread Ingredients

185g – 6oz Plain Flour
60g – 2oz Cornflour
125g – 4oz Caster Sugar
220g – 7oz Butter
½ Teaspoon Vanilla Extract

For the Ginger Icing

4 Tablespoons sifted Icing Sugar
30g – 1oz Butter
1½ Teaspoon Ground Ginger
3 Teaspoons Golden Syrup

*Baking Tin – 9" / 23cm x 1" / 2.5cm deep
(greased and lined)
Oven 180°C / 350°F / Gas Mark 4*

Place all the shortbread ingredients in the food processor and mix until a soft ball is formed.

Press into the lined baking dish. Smooth and prick the shortbread with a fork.

Cook for approximately 45-50 minutes or until a golden colour. Leave in the tin to cool.

Place all the icing ingredients in a saucepan over a low heat and stir continuously until blended together and boiling point is reached. Pour over the cooled shortbread and leave to set before cutting into portions.

NUTTY FLAPJACKS

Ingredients

185g – 6oz Butter

185g – 6oz Light Brown Sugar

2 Tablespoon Golden Syrup

375g – 12oz Porridge Oats

125g – 4oz Chopped Nuts – Brazil,
Pecan, Hazel Nuts or Almonds

A few extra nuts for decoration

*1 Lined Rectangular Baking Tin –
11" / 28cm x 6¹/₂" / 16cm
Moderate Oven 180°C / 350°F / Gas Mark 4*

Line the baking tin with Bakewell paper.

Melt together the butter, sugar and golden syrup. Add the porridge oats and nuts. Mix together thoroughly.

Press into the lined tin.

Bake in the centre of the oven for approximately 45-55 minutes.

Mark into fingers or squares and leave in the tin until cold.

The flapjacks are equally enjoyable served with morning coffee or afternoon tea.

GINGERBREAD PEOPLE

Ingredients

185g – 6oz Self-Raising Flour
125g – 4oz Plain Flour
1½ Tablespoons Ground Ginger
1½ Teaspoons Cinnamon
1 Good Pinch Ground Cloves
125g – 4oz Caster Sugar
3oz – 90g Butter
1 Egg
75ml (2¼ fl.oz) Golden Syrup
1 Tablespoon Black Treacle

Oven 180°C / 350°F / Gas Mark 4

Gingerbread Cutters

*Selection of Piping Bags
and Icing Colours*

Sift the flour and spices into a large bowl.

Stir in the caster sugar.

Cut the butter into small pieces and rub into the dry ingredients.

Mix the egg, golden syrup and treacle together.

Pour into the flour mixture and mix to a smooth dough.

Wrap in greaseproof paper and chill for 30 minutes in the refrigerator before using.

Roll out the gingerbread dough on a floured surface and cut out the gingerbread people with the appropriate cutters.

Transfer to the prepared baking sheets and bake for approximately 15-20 minutes.

Leave on the baking sheets for a short while before transferring to a wire rack to cool.

Decorate by piping different coloured icing.

Margaret's Recipes *From Her Tea Rooms*

CHOCOLATE ORANGE
BISCUIT

Ingredients

Shortbread Ingredients

375g – 12oz Plain Flour

250g – 8oz Butter

140g – 4¼ oz Caster Sugar

Grated Rind Of One Orange

Good Quality Chocolate of
your choice for coating

*Baking Tin – 9" / 23cm Diameter x 1" /
2.5cm deep (greased and lined)*

Oven 180°C / 350°F / Gas Mark 4

Place all the ingredients in a food
processor and mix until a soft ball is
formed.

Press into the lined baking dish. Smooth
and prick the shortbread with a fork.

Bake in the oven for approximately 30-35
minutes. Leave in the tin to cool.

Cover with melted chocolate
of your choice.

Cut into eight portions when the
chocolate has set.

DATE, APRICOT OR FIG SLICE

Ingredients

Shortbread Ingredients

375g – 12oz Plain Flour

250g – 8oz Butter

140g - 4½ oz Caster Sugar

250g – 8oz Dates, Apricots or Figs

1 x 9" / 23cm Diameter x 1½" / 3.5cm deep Tin – lined

Oven 180°C / 350°F / Gas Mark 4

Put all the ingredients into the food processor and mix until a soft ball is achieved.

Divide the mixture in half and roll out. Put the first half into the base of the lined tin. Cover with dates, apricots or figs.

Roll out the rest of the mixture and cover the fruit. Press down and smooth. Prick all over with a fork and divide into portions.

Bake in the oven for approximately 50-55 minutes.

Allow to cool before turning out of the tin.

Serve hot or cold, preferably with cream.

PLAIN SCONES

Ingredients

560g – 1lb 2oz Self-Raising Flour

2 Level Teaspoons Baking Powder

125g – 4oz Butter or Margarine

0g – 2oz Sugar – Granulated or Caster

2 Eggs – Beaten

Approx. 150ml / ¼ Pint Milk

*Oven 220°C / 450°F / Gas Mark 6
approximately 10-15 minutes*

*I always make my own jam to serve with
the scones in the Tea-Rooms.
The fresh dairy cream is delivered to us
daily from our local dairy.*

*If you don't manage to eat the scones
fresh on the day of baking, try them
toasted the next day. They are delicious
with butter and jam or lashings of
Norfolk Honey Butter.*

Place all the ingredients except the eggs and milk, in a food processor.

Mix for approximately 10 seconds.

Add the eggs and mix for a further 5 seconds.

Next, add the milk gradually until a soft ball is formed.

Turn the mixture onto a floured surface.

Pat down with floured hands and cut into 12 rounds, with a cutter.

Place the scones onto a lined baking tray.

Brush the tops lightly with milk and sprinkle with sugar.

Bake in a pre-heated oven for approx. 10-15 minutes or until golden brown.

Scones are always at their best when served straight from the oven.

Enjoy the scones served with butter, butter and jam or jam and fresh dairy cream.

NORFOLK HONEY BUTTER

Ingredients

250g – 8oz Soft Butter
2 Tablespoons Norfolk Honey
(preferably Set Honey)

In a medium sized bowl, blend the two ingredients together.

BASIC PLAIN SCONE –
Using an Electric Mixer

Ingredients

560g – 1lb 2oz Self-Raising Flour
2 Level Teaspoons Baking Powder
125g - 4oz Butter or Margarine
60g - 2oz Sugar – Granulated or Caster
2 Eggs – Beaten
Approx. ¼ Pint Milk

Oven 220°C / 450°F / Gas Mark 6

Place the flour and baking powder in the bowl, add the butter or margarine and mix on minimum speed until the fat is broken up. Increase the speed slightly until the fat is evenly distributed. Add the sugar and mix in thoroughly.

Reduce the speed to minimum; add the eggs and then the milk, a little at a time until a soft, pliable dough is formed.

Turn onto a lightly floured surface. Pat down with floured hands. Roll out to 1cm / ½ inch thickness and then cut out with a 2-inch cutter. Transfer to a baking tray lined with Bakewell paper. Brush the tops with milk and sprinkle a little sugar on top.

Bake towards the top of the oven 220°C / 450°F / Gas Mark 6 for approximately 10-15 minutes.

PLAIN SCONES –
Hand Method

Ingredients

560g – 1lb 2oz Self-Raising Flour

2 Level teaspoons Baking Powder

125g – 4oz Butter or Margarine

60g – 2oz Sugar – Granulated or Caster

2 Eggs – Beaten

Approx. ¼ Pint Milk

Large Baking Bowl
Oven 220°C / 450°F / Gas Mark 6

Sift flour and baking powder into a large baking bowl. Rub in the butter or margarine. Add the sugar. Mix to a soft dough with the beaten eggs and enough of the milk until pliable soft dough is formed. Turn onto a lightly floured board and knead quickly. Roll out to ½ inch thickness. Shape the scones with a knife or a 2-inch cutter. Place onto a lined baking tray, brush with milk and sprinkle with sugar.

Bake towards the top of the oven 220°C / 450° F / Gas Mark 6 for approximately 10-15 minutes, until golden. Delicious served with butter, jam or jam and cream.

Margaret's Recipes *From Her Tea Rooms*

NORFOLK SCONE

Ingredients

560g – 1lb 2oz Self-Raising Flour

2 Level Teaspoons Baking Powder

125g – 4oz Butter or Margarine

60g – 2oz Sugar – Granulated or Caster

2 Eggs – Beaten

Approx. 5 fluid oz / ¼ Pint Milk

For the Filling

90g – 3oz Soft Butter

60g – 2oz Soft Brown Sugar

315g – 10oz Mixed Fruit & Peel

4 Good Pinches Mixed Spice

Extra Milk and Sugar for the top

Oven 220°C / 450°F / Gas Mark 6
approximately 20-25 minutes

An extremely popular choice in the Tea-Rooms. At busy times, I have had problems keeping up with demand. Equally good with morning coffee or afternoon tea.

Place all the ingredients except the eggs and milk in a food processor.

Mix for approximately 10 seconds.

Add the eggs and mix for a further 5 seconds.

Next, add the milk gradually until a soft pliable dough is formed.

Turn the mixture onto a floured surface.

Pat down with floured hands.

Divide the scone in two and roll out to approximately ¼ inch thickness.

Place one half on to a large lined baking tray.

Spread with the soft butter. Spread the mixed fruit evenly on top of the butter.

Next sprinkle with the mixed spice.

Finally sprinkle the soft brown sugar.

Roll out the second half of the scone mixture and place on top.

Lightly coat the top with milk and then sprinkle the top with sugar.

Divide the top into portions.

Bake in the oven for approximately 20-25 minutes.

Turn the tray around during cooking.

If the top starts to brown too quickly, cover with a sheet of Bakewell paper.

Serve hot with a generous portion of thick cream.

LEMON/SULTANA SCONES

Ingredients

560g – 1lb 2oz Self-Raising Flour

2 Teaspoons Baking Powder

125g – 4oz Butter or Margarine

60g – 2oz Sugar

185g – 6oz Sultanas

Grated Rind of two Lemons

2 Eggs – beaten

Approx. 5 fluid oz / ¼ Pint of Milk

Oven 220°C / 450°F / Gas Mark 6
approximately 10-15 minutes

Place the flour, baking powder, butter or margarine, sugar and grated lemon rind in the food processor.

Mix for approximately 10 seconds.

Add the eggs and mix for a further 5 seconds.

Next, add enough of the milk gradually until a soft ball is formed.

Remove the processor bowl from its stand and gently fold in the sultanas.

Turn the mixture onto a floured surface.

Pat down with floured hands and cut into approx. 12 rounds with a cutter.

Place the scones onto a lined baking tray.

Brush the tops lightly with milk and sprinkle with sugar. This will give a nice crispy top.

Bake in a pre-heated oven for approx. 10-15 minutes or until golden brown.

Enjoy warm straight from the oven.
The fresh lemon flavour is delicious, especially served with butter.

I always enjoy experimenting with variations of flavours for scones; this one has proved to be very popular.

Margaret's Recipes *From Her Tea Rooms*

SPICY FRUIT SCONES

Ingredients

560g – 1lb 2oz Self-Raising Flour

2 Level Teaspoons Baking Powder

125g – 4oz Butter or Margarine

60g – 2oz Sugar – Granulated or Caster

2 Eggs – Beaten

Approx. 5 fluid oz / ¼ Pint Milk

185g – 6oz Mixed Fruit & Peel

½ Level Teaspoon Mixed Spice

Glacé Cherries (optional)

Oven 220°C / 450°F / Gas Mark 6
approximately 10-15 minutes

Place the flour, baking powder, butter, sugar and spice in the food processor.

Mix for approx. 10 seconds.

Add the eggs and mix for a further 5 seconds.

Next, add the milk gradually until a soft pliable dough is formed.

Remove the mixing bowl from the stand and gently fold in the mixed fruit.

Turn the mixture onto a floured surface.

Pat down with floured hands and cut into 12 rounds with a cutter.

Place the scones onto a lined baking tray.

Brush the tops lightly with milk and sprinkle with sugar.

A nice touch is to place a half glacé cherry on top of each scone.

Bake in a pre-heated oven for approx. 10-15 minutes or until golden brown.

Delicious eaten straight from the oven spread with butter.

I would not recommend jam to be served with these scones due to the spiciness.

Fruit scones are always a popular choice in the Tea-Rooms. It always pays to be generous with the fruit in scones.
One of my customers actually commented one day that it was nice not to have to play the game of searching for the currant!!!!

BANANA AND HAZELNUT SCONES

Ingredients

560g – 1lb 2oz Self-Raising Flour

2 Level Teaspoons Baking Powder

125g – 4oz Butter or Margarine

50g – 2oz Sugar – Granulated or Caster

2 Eggs – Beaten

1½ Peeled, fairly ripe Bananas

125g – 4oz Hazelnuts

+ 12 Hazelnuts for decoration

*Oven 220°C / 450°F / Gas Mark 6
approximately 10-15 minutes*

*As an alternative recipe, try banana
and Brazil nut or banana & date.*

Place the flour, baking powder, butter, sugar, banana and hazelnuts in the food processor.

Mix for approximately 10 seconds.

Gradually add the beaten eggs until a soft ball is formed.
(If the mixture remains dry, add a little milk until a soft pliable dough is formed. This usually isn't necessary, as the banana should substitute the milk.)

Turn the mixture onto a floured surface.

Pat down with floured hands and cut into 12 rounds with a cutter.

Place the scones onto a lined baking tray.

Coat the tops lightly with milk and sprinkle sugar on top. Place a hazelnut in the centre of each scone to decorate.

Bake in a pre-heated oven for approx. 10-15 minutes or until golden brown.

Enjoy straight from the oven served with butter or Norfolk Honey Butter.

STILTON AND WALNUT SCONES

Ingredients

560g – 1lb 2oz Self-Raising Flour

2 Teaspoons Baking Powder

125g – 4oz Butter

250g – 8oz Stilton Cheese

125g – 4oz Walnuts

2 Eggs – Beaten

Approx. 150ml / ¼ Pint Milk

+ extra Stilton and Broken Walnuts for decoration

Oven 220°C / 450°F / Gas Mark 6
approximately 15 minutes

Place the self-raising flour, baking powder, butter, stilton cheese and walnuts in a food processor.

Mix for approx. 10 seconds.

Add the eggs and mix for a further 5 seconds.

Next, add enough of the milk gradually, until a soft pliable dough is formed.

Turn the mixture onto a floured surface.

Pat down with floured hands and cut into 12 rounds with a cutter.

Place the scones onto a lined baking tray.

Spread the tops lightly with milk and place a small piece of stilton and broken walnut on top.

Bake in a pre-heated oven for approx. 15 minutes until they are nice and crispy.

For added flavour, add 2oz chopped apricots to this recipe.

If you really want to impress your friends or customers these are the scones to serve, especially with morning coffee. These have always been a great favourite with my gentlemen customers.

Margaret's Recipes *From Her Tea Rooms*

CHEESE/HERB SCONES

Ingredients

560gr – 1lb 2oz Self-Raising Flour

2 Teaspoons Baking Powder

125g – 4oz Butter or Margarine

2 Teaspoons Dried English Mustard

250g – 8oz Grated Strong Cheese (Cheddar
or Red Leicester give good results)

2 Teaspoons Dried Mixed Herbs (Thyme,
Parsley & Marjoram)

2 Eggs – Beaten

150ml / ¼ Pint Milk (approx.)

60g – 2oz Grated Cheese for the Topping

*Oven 220°C / 450°F / Gas Mark 6
approximately 10-15 minutes*

Place all the ingredients (except the eggs and milk) in the food processor.

Mix for approx. 10 seconds.

Add the eggs and mix for a further 5 seconds.

Next, add the milk gradually until a soft pliable dough is formed.

Turn the mixture onto a floured surface.

Pat down with floured hands and cut into 12 rounds with a cutter.

Place the scones onto a lined baking tray.

Spread the tops lightly with milk and place a small amount of grated cheese on the top.

Place in a pre-heated oven for approx. 10-15 minutes or until golden brown. Turn the baking tray in the oven during cooking.

Scones are always at their best when served straight from the oven.

Enjoy the scones served with butter.

If you don't manage to eat the scones fresh on the day of baking, try the cheese scones toasted with butter, grated cheese and pickle on top.
A nice mid-day snack, served with a side salad.

As an alternative recipe, try cheese & bacon scones.
Simply omit the herbs and add 125g / 4oz bacon.

Strawberry/Gooseberry Jam

Ingredients

1kg – 2lb Strawberries – fresh or frozen
500g – 1lb Gooseberries – fresh or frozen
1k 500g – 3lb Sugar
30g – 1oz Butter

One very large jam pan – 9 litres / 16 pints
Sterilised jam jars

*I cannot emphasize too strongly the care
that should be taken when making jam.*

Put the strawberries and gooseberries into the large jam pan and heat until boiling point is reached.

Squash the fruit and then carefully stir in the sugar and butter.

Return to the heat and bring back to boiling point.

Continue boiling for approx. 15-20 minutes or until setting point is reached. Very carefully stir the jam from time to time.

Ladle into the sterilised jars. Clean the rims and seal when cold.

Raspberry Or Loganberry Jam

Ingredients

1kg – 2lb Raspberries or
Loganberries (fresh or frozen)
1kg – 2lb Sugar
30g – 1oz Butter

One very large jam pan – 9 litre / 16 pints
Sterilised Jam Jars

Heat the raspberries in the large saucepan until boiling point is reached.

Carefully stir in the sugar and butter and mix well.

Bring back to boiling point and continue boiling for 10 minutes or until setting point is reached.

Ladle into the sterilised jars.

Clean the rims and seal when cold.

BLACKCURRANT/RHUBARB JAM

Ingredients

500g – 1lb Blackcurrants – fresh or frozen

500g – 1lb Chopped Rhubarb – fresh or frozen

300ml – ½ Pint Water

1kg – 2lb Sugar

30g – 1oz Butter

One very large jam pan – 9 litres / 16 pints
Sterilised Jam Jars

Put the blackcurrants, rhubarb and water into the large saucepan and heat to boiling point.

Carefully add the sugar and butter and stir well.

Return to the heat and bring back to boiling point.

Continue cooking for approx. 5-10 minutes or until setting point is reached.

Ladle the jam into the sterilised jars and seal when cold.

43

APRICOT JAM

Ingredients

1kg – 2lb Dried Apricot (pre-soaked)
750ml – 1¼ Pints Water
2kg – 4lb Sugar
Juice of 1 Lemon

One very large jam pan –
9 litres / 16 pints
Sterilised Jam Jars

Chop the apricots very finely, either by hand or in the food processor.

Place the apricots, water and lemon juice into the large saucepan and bring to the boil.

Carefully add the sugar and stir well until the sugar has dissolved.

Bring back to the boil, stirring from time to time.

Reduce the heat and continue cooking for approx. 30 minutes.

Continue to stir the jam at regular intervals.

Ladle the jam into the sterilised jars. Clean the rims and seal well when cold.

PINEAPPLE JAM

Ingredients

2kg – 4lb Fresh Pineapple –
cut into small pieces

1½ Litres Water

Juice of 3 Lemons

2kg – 4lb Sugar

*One very large jam pan –
9 litres / 16 pints*

Put the pineapple, water and lemon juice into the large saucepan. Heat the fruit until boiling point is reached and continue to simmer for approx. one hour.

Carefully stir in the sugar until dissolved.

Return the pan to the heat and bring back to boiling point.

Continue to boil for approx. 30 minutes or until setting point is reached.

Ladle the jam into the sterilised jars and seal when cold.

45

MAG'S ENGLISH MUFFINS

Ingredients

1kg 500g – 3lb Strong Plain
White Flour

3 Teaspoons Salt
1 Teaspoon Sugar
30g – 1oz Butter or Margarine
45g – 1½ oz Fresh Yeast
900ml – 1½ Pints Tepid Milk

*This recipe will make 24 muffins.
Reduce the ingredients
for smaller quantities but follow
the same instructions.*

*Medium Heat Griddle –
15 minutes each side*

Into a mixer bowl pour in the milk.

Add the sugar and crumble in the fresh yeast.

Add the butter or margarine, flour and salt.

Using a dough hook knead all the ingredients together for approximately one minute on the minimum speed.

Increase the speed until a dough is formed, adding a little more flour if necessary.

Knead for a further 2-3 minutes until the dough is smooth and elastic and leaves the sides of the bowl clean.

Place the dough in a very large dish or polythene bag and leave somewhere warm to double in size, about 1-1½ hours.

Return to the bowl and knead again for about 2 minutes.

Divide the dough into 24 pieces and shape into buns on a well floured board. Place them on Bakewell paper-covered baking trays, well apart. Leave in a warm place until doubled in size.

Place the muffins a few at a time on to a medium heat, lightly oiled griddle and cook for about 15 minutes each side.

Cool on a wire rack.

When ready to eat, slice down the middle and toast the centres. Delicious served hot with butter and home-made jam.

SPICY TEACAKES

Ingredients

Naturally, when I make the bread and teacakes for the Tea-Rooms I have to work in fairly large quantities. This recipe will make 24 teacakes (of course, I have to use very large mixing bowls and dough hooks).

For small quantities use the domestic size mixer and dough hook and reduce the quantities to one third of the following:

1k 500g – 3lb Strong White Flour
3 Teaspoons Salt
2 Teaspoons Sugar
30g – 1oz Margarine or Butter
30g – 1oz Fresh Yeast
500g – 1lb Mixed Vine Fruits and Peel
4 Teaspoons Mixed Spice
900ml – 1½ Pints Milk (luke warm)

*Four baking trays lined with Bakewell paper
Oven 220°C / 450°F / Gas Mark 6*

Put the flour, salt, sugar, margarine, yeast, and milk into a very large mixing bowl.

Using a dough hook on a low setting mix all the ingredients together.

When thoroughly mixed leave the mixer running to allow the dough hook to knead the dough for about three minutes until soft and pliable.

Transfer to a large bowl. Cover and leave in a warm place until well risen.

Once risen, transfer back to the mixing bowl to knock down using the dough hook for approximately two minutes.

Add the fruit and mixed spice and mix again for a further minute or so until they are well combined.

Transfer the dough to a floured surface. Knead by hand for a while and then cut into 24 more or less equal portions. Place them onto the baking trays and leave to rise in a warm place for approximately ½ - 1 hour.

Cook in the hot oven for approximately 10 minutes, turning the tray during cooking.

Serve hot straight from the oven with butter or allow to cool and serve toasted, with butter.

Is anything in the world as satisfying as the smell of bread cooking?

HOME-MADE MINCEMEAT

Ingredients

250g – 8oz Mixed Vine Fruits (Currants,
Sultanas, Raisins and Dried Mixed Peel)

125g – 4oz Shredded Suet
(use Vegetarian Suet if preferred)

125g – 4oz Almonds – Chopped
1 Large Granny Smith Apple, Peeled,
Cored and Grated

Juice and Grated Rind of two Lemons
Juice and Grated Rind of one Orange
60g – 2oz Soft Brown Sugar
1 Teaspoon Mixed Spice
60ml – 2fl.oz Brandy

1 Large Mixing Bowl
Sterilised Jam Jars

Place all the ingredients into the
large bowl and mix well.

Spoon into sterilised jars and seal
the lids tightly.

Store until required.

Best left for at least one week
before use.

Bread Basket

BASIC BREAD RECIPE

Ingredients

1kg 500g – 3lb Strong Plain Flour

3 Teaspoons Salt

1 Teaspoon Sugar

30g – 1oz Butter or Margarine

45g – 1½ oz Fresh Yeast

900ml – 1½ Pints Luke Warm Milk

Cook at 220°C / 450°F / Gas Mark 6
30-35 minutes

Into a mixer bowl pour in the milk, add the sugar and crumble in the fresh yeast. Add the butter or margarine, flour and salt.

Using a dough hook knead all the ingredients together for approximately one minute on the minimum speed.

Increase the speed until a dough is formed, adding a little more flour if necessary.

Knead for a further 2-3 minutes until the dough is smooth and elastic and leaves the sides of the bowl clean.

Place the dough in a very large dish or polythene bag and leave somewhere warm to double in size, about 1-1½ hours.

Return to the bowl and knead again for about 2 minutes.

Divide the mixture into 4 x 500g/1lb greased tins
(which should be half-full).

Leave the loaves to prove, until doubled in size.

Cook for 30-35 minutes.

When cooked the loaves should sound hollow when tapped on the bottom.

As an alternative to white bread, follow the same instructions using a selection of different flours, i.e. wholemeal, wheatcraft or spelt.

For a lighter loaf, use one-third white flour with the wholemeal, wheatcraft or spelt.

Have fun making different shape loaves, i.e. cottage loaves or plaits. Decorate the tops by coating with a mixture of egg and milk and sprinkling with poppy seeds, sesame seeds or sunflower seeds.

WALNUT, PECAN NUT OR BRAZIL NUT BREAD

Ingredients

(This recipe will make two 500g / 1lb loaves)

500g – 1lb Strong White Plain Flour
1 Level Teaspoon Salt
½ Teaspoon Sugar
15g – ½ oz Fresh Yeast
15g – ½ oz Margarine or Butter
150ml – ¼ Pint Milk and 150ml / ¼ Pint Hot Water
(combined to make 300ml / ½ Pint Tepid Liquid)

500g – 1lb Wholemeal, Spelt or Granary Flour
1 Level Teaspoon Salt
½ Teaspoon Sugar
15g – ½ oz Fresh Yeast
15g – ½ oz Margarine or Butter
150g – ¼ Pint Milk and 150ml / ¼ Pint Hot Water
(combined to make 300ml / ½ Pint Tepid Liquid)

Two 1lb Bread Tins (greased and floured)
Cook at 220°C / 450°F / Gas Mark 6

Into a mixer bowl pour in the combined milk and water

Add the sugar and crumble in the fresh yeast.

Add the butter or margarine, white flour and salt.

Using a dough hook, knead all the ingredients together for approximately one minute on the minimum speed. Increase the speed until a dough is formed, adding a little more flour if necessary.

Knead for a further 2-3 minutes until the dough is smooth and elastic and leaves the sides of the bowl clean

Place the dough in a very large dish or polythene bag and leave somewhere warm to double in size.
About 1-1½ hours.

Return to the bowl and knead again for about 2 minutes

For the second loaf, repeat the instructions as above using the wholemeal, spelt or granary flour instead of the white flour.

When both loaves are ready to shape, cut each one in half.

On a floured surface place the first half white dough on top of the first half brown dough and roll out with a rolling pin.

Cover the surface with the nuts. Roll the dough and press down firmly in the bread tin. Repeat the process with the second two halves.

Leave the loaves to prove, until doubled in size.

Cook for 30-35 minutes.

Margaret's Recipes *From Her Tea Rooms*

Margaret's Recipes *From Her Tea Rooms*

STILTON, APRICOT & WALNUT LOAVES

Ingredients

(This recipe will make two 500g / 1lb loaves)

500g – 1lb Strong White Plain Flour
1 Level Teaspoon Salt
½ Teaspoon Sugar
15g – ½ oz Fresh Yeast
15g – ½ oz Margarine or Butter
150ml / ¼ Pint Milk and 150ml / ¼ Pint Hot Water
(combined to make 300ml / ½ Pint Tepid Liquid)

500g – 1lb Wholemeal, Spelt or Granary Flour
1 Level Teaspoon Salt
½ Teaspoon Sugar
15g – ½ oz Fresh Yeast
15g – ½ oz Margarine or Butter
150ml / ¼ Pint Milk and 150ml / ¼ Pint Hot Water
(combined to make 300ml / ½ Pint Tepid Liquid)

185g-250g – 6-8oz Stilton Cheese
125g-185g – 4-6oz Pre-Soaked Apricots
125g – 4oz Broken Walnuts

Cook at 220°C / 450°F / Gas Mark 6

Into a mixer bowl pour in the combined milk and water.

Add the sugar and crumble in the fresh yeast.

Add the butter or margarine, white flour and salt.

Using a dough hook knead all the ingredients together for approximately one minute on the minimum speed. Increase the speed until a dough is formed, adding a little more flour if necessary.

Knead for a further 2-3 minutes until the dough is smooth and elastic and leaves the sides of the bowl clean.

Place the dough in a very large dish or polythene bag and leave somewhere warm to double in size for about 1-1½ hours.

Return to the mixer and knead again for about 2 minutes.

For the second loaf, repeat the instructions as above using the wholemeal, spelt or granary flour instead of the white flour.

When both the loaves are ready to shape, cut each one in half.

On a floured surface place the first half white dough on top of the first half brown dough and roll out with a rolling pin.

Cover the surface with the stilton cheese and arrange the apricots and walnuts in stripes. Roll the dough and press down firmly in the bread tin. Repeat the process with the second two halves.

Leave the loaves to prove, until doubled in size. Cook for 30-35 minutes.

CHEESE & SUN DRIED TOMATO BREAD

Ingredients

Sliced Black Olives (optional)

500g – 1lb Strong White Plain Flour

1 Level Teaspoon Salt

½ Teaspoon Sugar

15g – ½ oz Fresh Yeast

15g – ½ oz Margarine or Butter

150ml / ¼ Pint Milk and 150ml /
¼ Pint Hot Water (combined to make 300ml /
½ Pint Tepid Liquid)

500g – 1lb Wholemeal, Spelt or Granary Flour

1 Level Teaspoon Salt

½ Teaspoon Sugar

15g – ½ oz Fresh Yeast

15g – ½ oz Margarine or Butter

150ml / ¼ Pint Milk and 150ml /
¼ Pint Hot Water (combined to make 300ml /
½ Pint Tepid Liquid)

250g – 8oz Strong Flavoured Grated Cheese
(Cheddar or Red Leicester always work well)

125g-185g – 4-6oz Sun Dried Tomatoes

Cook at 220°C / 450°F / Gas Mark 6

Into a mixer bowl pour in the combined milk and water.

Add the sugar and crumble in the fresh yeast.

Add the butter or margarine, white flour and salt.

Using the dough hook knead all the ingredients together for approximately one minute on the minimum speed. Increase the speed until a dough is formed, adding a little more flour if necessary.

Knead for a further 2-3 minutes until the dough is smooth and elastic and leaves the sides of the bowl clean.

Place the dough in a very large dish or polythene bag and leave somewhere warm to double in size, for about 1-1½ hours.

Return to the mixer and knead again for about 2 minutes.

For the second loaf, repeat the instructions as above using the wholemeal, spelt or granary flour instead of the white flour.

When both the loaves are ready to shape, cut each one in half.

On a floured surface place the first half white dough on top of the first half brown dough and roll out with a rolling pin.

Cover the surface with the grated cheese and arrange the sun dried tomatoes over the cheese. Roll the dough and press down firmly in the bread tin. Repeat the process with the second two halves.

Leave the loaves to prove, until doubled in size. Cook for 30-35 minutes.

For added flavour spread one tablespoon of sliced black olives over the cheese with the sun-dried tomatoes.

Savoury Lunch

MUSHROOM AND PECAN NUT SOUP

Ingredients

2 Large Onions

1 Teaspoon Olive Oil

60g – 2oz Butter

1k 500g – 3lb Mushrooms

125g – 4oz Pecan Nuts

4 Vegetable Stock Cubes

½ Teaspoon Salt

¼ Teaspoon Black Pepper

Approx. 2 Pints Water

600ml / 1 Pint Milk

Single Cream for garnish
A few extra mushrooms, sliced for garnish

Melt the butter and olive oil in a large saucepan and sauté the onions until transparent.

Add the mushrooms, followed by the pecan nuts, stock cubes, seasoning and water.

Bring to the boil and then reduce the heat. Continue to simmer for approx. 10-15 minutes until the mushrooms are well cooked.

Allow to cool slightly before liquidising the soup.

During the liquidising process, add the milk.

Reheat to serving temperature and adjust the seasoning to taste.

Garnish with a swirl of cream and a few slices of mushroom.

PARSNIP & APPLE SOUP

Ingredients

30g – 1oz Butter or Margarine

1 Teaspoon Olive Oil

2 Large Onions – sliced

1k 500g – 3lb Parsnips – peeled and chopped

2 Large Cooking Apples – peeled and cored

900ml / 1½ Pints Water

3 Vegetable Stock Cubes

Good Pinch Salt and Ground Pepper

Single Cream

Melt the butter with the olive oil in a large saucepan.

Add the onion and cook gently for 2-3 minutes.

Add the parsnips and apples and cook until they begin to soften.

Pour the water over the vegetables.

Stir in the stock cubes and add the seasoning.

Continue to simmer until all the vegetables are fully cooked.

Liquidise the soup and return to a clean saucepan.

The soup can be prepared in advance but when ready to use, reheat and just before boiling point is reached, remove from the heat and add the single cream to taste.

Serve with a thick slice of home-made bread or as an alternative to bread, try a buttered savoury scone.

CAULIFLOWER AND STILTON SOUP

Ingredients

30g – 1oz Butter or Margarine

1 Teaspoon Olive Oil

2 Medium Cauliflowers
(washed and stalks removed)

2 Large Onions – peeled and sliced

4 Large Potatoes – peeled and sliced

Sufficient Water to cover the vegetables

3 Vegetable Stock Cubes

Salt and Pepper to taste

Approx. 250g – 8oz Stilton Cheese

Single Cream – to taste

Melt the butter with the olive oil in a large saucepan.

Add the onions and cook gently for 2-3 minutes.

Add the cauliflower and potatoes.

Sprinkle the stock cubes over the vegetables and then add the water

Continue to simmer until all the vegetables are well cooked.

Add the salt and pepper.

Liquidise the soup and return to a clean saucepan.

Add more stock for a thinner consistency.

Reheat the soup and add some single cream and Stilton cheese just
before boiling point is reached.

Serve the soup and garnish with extra single cream, parsley and
another piece of Stilton cheese.

CARROT & ORANGE SOUP

Ingredients

2 Large Onions

1kg – 2lb Carrots

900ml / 1½ Pints Water

3 Vegetable Stock Cubes

Rind and Juice of one medium Orange

60g – 2oz Butter

2 Teaspoons Olive Oil

Good Pinch of Salt and Black Pepper

Melt the butter and olive oil in a large saucepan and sauté the onion until transparent.

Add the roughly chopped carrots, followed by the orange rind and juice.

Season well. Finally add the stock cubes and water.

Bring to the boil and then reduce the heat. Simmer for approx. 30 minutes until the carrots are well cooked.

Allow to cool slightly before liquidising the soup.

Reheat to serving temperature and adjust the seasoning to taste.

BACON & EGG PIE

Ingredients

750g - 1½ lb Golden Jewel or Plain Flour

375g – 12oz Butter

Cold Water to mix

10 Rashers of Lean Bacon

8 Eggs

1 Heaped Teaspoon Mixed Herbs

+ 1 Egg – Beaten

*Greased Baking Tin or Pyrex Dish –
10" / 25cm diameter x 1½" / 3.5cm deep*

*Oven 200°C / 400°F / Gas Mark 5
for 1 hour, plus*

*Oven 160°C / 325°F / Gas Mark 3
for half an hour*

*As an alternative, make a sausage, bacon & egg
pie by spreading 1lb sausage meat on the pastry
base before the first five rashers of bacon.*

*Another alternative would be to omit
the eggs and fill the pie with sausage meat,
cooking apples and bacon.*

Place the flour and butter in the food processor.

Mix well for a few seconds and then add enough cold water gradually to form a fairly soft dough. Place the dough in the fridge for about half an hour. Roll out half the pastry and line the tin or dish. Trim around the edge. Cover the base of the pastry with five rashers of bacon.

Break the eight eggs into a basin. **Do not beat the eggs.**

Carefully pour the eggs over the bacon and sprinkle with the mixed herbs (optional).

Place the remaining five rashers of bacon over the eggs.

Roll out the remaining pastry and use to cover the pie. Seal the edges well. Coat the top of the pie evenly with the beaten egg.

Any remaining pastry can be used to cut out shapes if you wish to decorate the top of the pie.

Place the pie dish on to a baking tray and place in the oven.

Cook for approximately 1 hour and then reduce the heat to 160°C for a further half hour. Or until well cooked.

Cover the top of the pie with Bakewell paper during cooking to prevent it browning too quickly.

Serve hot or cold.

Stilton, Apricot & Walnut Flan

Ingredients

Pastry Ingredients

500g – 1lb Golden Jewel or Plain Flour
125g – 4oz Butter or Margarine
125g – 4oz White Flora
Cold Water for Mixing

440g – 14oz Chopped Stilton Cheese
185g – 6oz Broken Walnuts
185g – 6oz Pre-Soaked Apricots

4 Eggs – Beaten
rox. 300ml/ ½ Pint Single Cream or Milk

Pyrex Dish or Baking Tin – 10" /
25cm diameter x 1½" / 3.5cm deep

Oven 200°C / 400°F / Gas Mark 5
1 hour 15 minutes

To make the Pastry

Place the flour, butter or margarine and White Flora in the food processor.

Mix well for a few seconds and then add enough cold water gradually, until a fairly soft pastry dough is formed.
Place the dough in the fridge for about half an hour.

Roll out the pastry and line the greased baking tin or Pyrex dish.

Spread the Stilton cheese evenly over the base of the pastry. Next, cover the Stilton with the apricots and finally sprinkle the chopped walnuts on top.

Beat the eggs well in a large jug and add the cream to a level of approximately ¾ Pint. Pour over the Stilton etc. and place on a baking tray. Cook in the oven for approx.
1 hour 15 minutes. When the flan starts to brown on top cover with a sheet of Bakewell paper.

65

ROAST VEGETABLE &
CHEESE FLAN

Ingredients

500g – 1lb Golden Jewel or Plain Flour

125g – 4oz Butter or Margarine

125g – 4oz White Flora

Cold Water for Mixing

1 Red, Yellow and Green Pepper

2 Medium Onions

3 Medium Sized Potatoes

2 Courgettes, 1 Aubergine,

1 Large Carrot

2 Tablespoons Olive Oil

4 Eggs – Beaten

300ml / ½ Pint Single Cream

250g – 8oz Grated Cheese (*Cheddar,*
Red Leicester or Double Gloucester all make
good choices, or even a mixture of all three)

Baking Tin or Pyrex Dish –
10" / 25cm diameter x 1½" / 3.5cm deep

To make the Pastry

Place the flour, butter and White Flora in the food processor.
Mix for a few seconds and add enough cold water gradually until a
fairly soft pastry dough is formed. Place the pastry in the fridge for
about half an hour.

Wash and prepare all the vegetables. Roughly, chop and place the
vegetables in a roasting tin. Season well and sprinkle with the olive o

Roast in a hot oven 220°C / 450°F / Gas Mark 5 for approximately
45 minutes. Remove from the oven and allow to cool a little.

In the meantime, line the baking tin with the pastry. Trim the edges

Place all the roasted vegetables into the pastry case.

Beat the eggs well in a large jug and add the cream to a level of ¾
Pour over the vegetables and sprinkle the cheese on top.

Place the dish onto a baking tray. Bake in the oven for
approximately 1 hour or until set and the pastry is well cooked.

Cover with Bakewell paper half way through cooking in order to
prevent the cheese from becoming overcooked.

66

CRANBERRY, CHICKEN & ALMOND FLAN

Ingredients

Pastry Ingredients

500g – 1lb Golden Jewel or Plain Flour
250g – 8oz Butter
Cold Water for Mixing

4 Tablespoons Cranberry Sauce
500g – approx. 1lb Cooked Chicken
cut into small cubes
100g – 4oz Flaked Almonds
4 Eggs – Beaten

Approx. 300ml /
½ Pint Single Cream or Milk

Baking Tin or Pyrex Dish –
0" / 25cm diameter x 1½" / 3.5cm deep

Oven 220°C / 450°F / Gas Mark 5
Cooking Time approximately 1 Hour

To make the Pastry

Place the flour and butter in the food processor.

Mix well for a few seconds and then add enough cold water gradually to form a fairly soft dough. Place the dough in the fridge for about half an hour.

Roll out the pastry and line the baking tin or Pyrex dish. Spread the cranberry sauce evenly over the base of the pastry.

Arrange the chicken over the cranberry sauce and sprinkle the almonds over the top of the chicken.

Beat the eggs well in a large jug and add the cream or milk up to three quarters of a pint. Pour into the flan case carefully.

Stand the dish onto a baking sheet and place carefully in the oven.

Cook for approximately one hour, until the flan is set and the pastry well cooked. Cover the top with Bakewell paper halfway through cooking, in order to prevent the almonds from becoming overcooked.

Stand for a while to allow the flan to settle. Best served hot straight from the oven.

SMOKED SALMON &
SPINACH FLAN

Ingredients

500g – 1lb Golden Jewel or Plain Flour

125g – 4oz Butter or Margarine

125g – 4oz White Flora

Cold Water to mix

1lb Smoked Salmon or use tinned Salmon
as an alternative

80g Bag of Baby Spinach

(available from most Supermarkets)

Pinch of Salt

Approx. half Pint Single Cream or Milk

4 Eggs – Beaten

*Baking Tin or Pyrex Dish –
10" / 25cm diameter x 1¹/₂" / 3.5cm deep*

*Oven 220°C / 450°F / Gas Mark 6
Approx. 1 hour 15 minutes*

Boil a small amount of water in a saucepan. Add the baby spinach and a pinch of salt. Cook for approximately one minute. Drain the spinach and leave to one side to cool.

To make the pastry. Place the flour, butter or margarine and White Flora in the food processor. Mix well for a few seconds and then add enough water to form a fairly soft dough. Place in the fridge for about half an hour.

Roll out the pastry and line the baking tin. Trim the edges.

Line the base of the pastry with the smoked salmon.

Beat the eggs and cream together in a large measuring jug, these should measure up to ¾ pint. Add the cooked spinach and continue to beat together.

Pour the mixture over the salmon.

Put the dish onto a baking tray and place in the oven. Cook for approximately 1 hour 15 minutes, ensuring that it is properly set and the pastry well cooked.

Half way through the cooking process, cover with a sheet of Bakewell paper to prevent it from becoming too brown on top.

Allow the flan to stand for a short while before serving.

Enjoy hot or cold.

69

SALMON & CHEESE FLAN

Ingredients

500g – 1lb Golden Jewel or Plain Flour
125g – 4oz Butter or Margarine
125g – 4oz White Flora
Cold Water to mix

For the Filling

500g – 1lb Smoked Salmon or Tinned Salmon
4 Eggs – (Well Beaten)
Approx. 300ml / ½ Pint Single Cream or Milk
¼ Teaspoon Nutmeg
250g – 8oz Grated Cheese (Cheddar, Red Leicester or any hard Cheese of your choice)

*Baking Tin or Pyrex Dish –
10" / 25cm diameter x 1½" / 3.5cm deep.*

*Oven 200°C / 400°F / Gas Mark 5
approximately 1 hour 15 minutes*

Place the flour, butter and White Flora in the food processor. Mix well for a few seconds and then add enough cold water gradually to form a fairly soft dough. Place the dough in the fridge for about half an hour.

Roll out the pastry and line the baking tin. Trim the edges.

Cover the base of the pastry with the salmon.

Beat the eggs and cream together. Add the nutmeg and mix thoroughly.

Pour the mixture over the salmon and sprinkle the cheese on top.

Stand the dish on a baking tray and place in the oven. Cook for approximately 1 hour 15 minutes.

When the top begins to brown cover with a sheet of Bakewell paper to prevent the cheese from burning.

When cooked, allow to stand for a short while before dividing into portions. These can be served hot or cold.

Desserts

FIG CUSTARD TART

Ingredients

500g – 1lb Golden Jewel Flour

125g – 4oz Butter or Margarine

125g – 4oz White Flora

Enough Cold Water to mix to a fairly soft consistency

For the Filling

375g – 12oz pre-soaked Figs

8 Egg Yolks

1 Pint Cream or Milk

90g – 3oz Caster Sugar

Grated Nutmeg

Glass Flan Dish – 10" / 25cm diameter x 1¹/₂" / 3.5cm deep

Oven 200°C / 450°F / Gas Mark 5 approximately one hour

Place the flour, butter and Flora into the food processor. Mix for a few second until it resembles fine breadcrumbs.

Pour in the water gradually until a fairly soft ball is formed.

Line the greased flan dish with the pastry and place in the fridge for ¹/₂ hour.

In the meantime, beat the egg yolks and sugar together.

Heat the cream or milk until nearly boiling point. Cover the pastry case with the figs. Place the flan dish onto a baking tray.

Pour the cream over the egg and sugar mix and beat thoroughly. Pour over the figs and sprinkle enough nutmeg to taste over the top.

Carefully place in the oven for approximately 60 minutes until the custard is set. Cover the top with Bakewell paper. Lower the oven temperature. Transfe the tart to the bottom of the oven for approximately 30 minutes to ensure the pastry is cooked at the bottom.

As an alternative to figs, use apricots or dates in this recipe.

PECAN PIE

Ingredients

500g – 1lb Golden Jewel Flour (or Plain Flour)
125g – 4oz Butter or Margarine
125g – 4oz White Flora
(Enough Cold Water to mix to a fairly soft consistency)

For the Filling

90g – 3oz Butter
220g – 7oz Soft Light Brown Sugar
6 Fluid Ounces Maple Syrup
2 Tablespoons Golden Syrup
4 Eggs – Beaten
2 Teaspoons Ground Cinnamon
375g – 12oz Pecan Nuts

Glass Pyrex Flan Dish – 10" / 25cm diameter x
1¹/₂" / 3.5cm deep

Oven 180°C / 350°F / Gas Mark 4
approximately 1¹/₂ -1³/₄ hours

Make the pastry by mixing the pastry ingredients in the food processor. Line the flan dish with the pastry and stand the dish on a baking tray.

Cream the butter and sugar together. Add the maple syrup and golden syrup and mix well.

Next, add the beaten eggs and cinnamon.

Finally add the pecan nuts and mix thoroughly before pouring into the pastry case.

Carefully transfer to the oven and cook until the mixture sets. You may need to cover with Bakewell/or greaseproof paper during cooking to prevent the top from burning.

As an alternative to pecan nuts, use mixed nuts or a mixture of dates and walnuts.

All very delicious, best served hot with fresh pouring cream or ice cream.

As an alternative to pecan nuts, try using 375g – 12oz walnuts, or 375g – 12oz mixed nuts or 185g – 6oz dates and 185g – 6oz walnuts.

When the nuts begin to brown on top cover with a double sheet or greaseproof paper.

ALMOND BAKEWELL TART

Ingredients

Pastry Ingredients

500g – 1lb Golden Jewel Flour

125g – 4oz Margarine

125g – 4oz White Flora

Cold Water to mix

Strawberry Jam – approximately 2 Tablespoons

Sponge Mixture Ingredients

185g – 6oz Margarine or Butter

185g – 6oz Sugar *(Granulated or Caster)*

185g – 6oz Self-Raising Flour

1 Teaspoon Baking Powder

3 Large Eggs

1 Teaspoon Almond Extract

125g – 4oz Flaked Almonds to
decorate the top *(optional)*

*Large Pyrex Dish –
10" / 25cm diameter x 1½" / 3.5cm deep*

*Oven 180°C / 350°F / Gas Mark 4
55-60 minutes or until well cooked*

Combine all the pastry ingredients in the food processor until a soft ball is formed.

Roll out the pastry and line the greased Pyrex dish.

Spread the pastry base with the strawberry jam.

Combine all the sponge ingredients in the food processor, knocking down during mixing. When a nice soft consistency is reached, pour into the pastry case. Scatter the flaked almonds on top to decorate.

Bake in the centre of the oven for approximately 1½ hours until well cooked. Cover with greaseproof paper to prevent it from browning too quickly on top.

Delicious served hot or cold with cream, ice cream or custard.

QUICK ALMOND PUDDING

Ingredients

1 Packet Frozen Flaky Pastry
3 Tablespoons Strawberry Jam
(preferably Home-made)
125g – 4oz Butter
185g – 6oz Caster Sugar
6 Egg Yolks
3 Egg Whites
90g – 3oz Ground Almonds
1 Teaspoon Almond Extract

Large Pyrex Dish –
10" / 25cm diameter x 1¹/₂" / 3.5cm deep
Oven 200°C / 400°F / Gas Mark 5
approximately 40-50 minutes

Defrost the frozen pastry at room temperature.

Roll out the pastry. Line the Pyrex dish with the pastry.
Spread this with the strawberry jam.

Melt together the butter and sugar and mix well.

Carefully blend in the egg yolks and whites and to this add
the ground almonds and the almond extract.

Mix thoroughly and pour over the jam into the pastry case.

Bake in a hot oven for approximately 40-50 minutes.
If the top becomes brown before the centre is set, cover
with Bakewell paper.

Delicious served hot with fresh pouring cream.

My husband Roger is not one for puddings and sweets
normally but he never says 'no' to this one, it's his favourite.

75

FRUIT PIES

Ingredients

To make the Pastry
500g – 1lb Golden Jewel or Plain Flour
125g – 4oz Butter or Margarine
125g – 4oz White Flora
Cold Water for mixing

Apple & Apricot Pie
500g – 1lb Pre-soaked Apricots
3 Large Cooking Apples
1 Tablespoon Cornflour

Pyrex Dish - 9¹/₂" / 24cm diameter

Oven 220°C / 450°F / Gas Mark 6
50-60 minutes

Place the flour, butter and White Flora in the food processor.

Mix for a few seconds and add enough cold water gradually, until a fairly soft pastry dough is formed. Place the pastry in the fridge for about half an hour. Roll out the pastry and line the greased Pyrex dish.

In the meantime prepare the fruit for the pie.

Peel and core the apples. Part cook the apples and pour away any surplus juice. Add the pre-soaked apricots and mix well with the apples. Add one tablespoon sugar and one tablespoon cornflour and continue to mix.

Place the prepared fruit into the pastry base.

Roll out the remaining pastry and place the top on the pie. Trim and shape the edges.

Bake in the centre of the oven for approximately 50-60 minutes.

Pies are an excellent way to use fruits from the freezer as well as using fresh seasonal fruits.

Other fruit pie suggestions may include:

- Apple & Blackcurrant (1kg – 2lb Apples, 500g – 1lb Blackcurrants, 2 Tablespoons Sugar & 1 Tablespoon Cornflour)

- Gooseberry & Strawberry (1kg – 2lb Gooseberries, 500g – 1lb Strawberries, 2 Tablespoons Sugar & 1 Tablespoon Cornflour)

- Gooseberry & Apricot (1kg – 2lb Gooseberries & 500g – 1lb Apricots, 1 Tablespoon Sugar & 1 Tablespoons Cornflour)

- Apple & Plum (1kg – 2lb Apples & 500g – 1lb Plums, 1 Tablespoon Sugar and 1 Cornflour)

- Apple & Raspberry or Loganberry (1kg – 2lb Apples & 500g – 1lb Raspberries, 1 Tablespoon Sugar & 1 Cornflour)

- Blackcurrant & Rhubarb (1kg – 2lb Blackcurrants & 500g – 1lb Rhubarb, 2 Tablespoons Sugar & 1 Cornflour)

SHORTCRUST PASTRY –
Hand Method

Ingredients

1 lb Golden Jewel or Plain Flour

Pinch of Salt (*optional*)

4oz. Butter or Margarine

4oz White Flora

Approx. 8 Tablespoons cold water, to mix

Oven 220° C / 450° F / Gas Mark 6

Sift the flour and salt into a cold mixing bowl. Cut the butter and Flora into the flour with a round-bladed knife and coat the small pieces of fat with the flour. Rub the fat into the flour, lifting the mixture up with both hands.

Continue rubbing in until the mixture resembles fine breadcrumbs. Sprinkle the cold water over gradually and mix in with a round-bladed knife, or palette knife, until the mixture begins to form lumps, which leave the side of the bowl cleanly. Knead the dough together lightly with a cool hand.

SHORTCRUST PASTRY –
Using an Electric Mixer

Sift the flour and Salt into the bowl of the electric mixer. Then add the butter and White Flora. Cut into small cubes. Using a K-Beater or pastry mixer, turn the machine on at minimum speed and increase gradually to speed 2 as the fats break up, then continue mixing at speed 2 until the mixture resembles fine breadcrumbs (about 2 minutes). Add cold water gradually, and mix at speed 2 until the mixture forms a dough that leaves the sides of the bowl clean. Turn the mixer off immediately.

Turn the dough onto a lightly floured pastry board and knead very lightly with clean, cool hands until smooth. Pat into a round cake shape. Wrap in greaseproof paper and chill in the refrigerator for 30 minutes before use.

MINCEMEAT GALETTE

Ingredients

For a very quick and easy 'Pudding' here is an opportunity to cheat a little.

You will need:

One Packet of Frozen Flaky Pastry
One Jar of Home-Made Mincemeat or
One Jar of Good Brand Commercial Mincemeat

Oven 220°C / 450°F / Gas Mark 6
20-25 minutes

Roll out half the pastry into a rectangle shape.

Place on Bakewell paper on a baking tray.

Spread the mincemeat on top leaving an edge of approximately ½ inch all the way round.

Roll out another rectangle with the remaining pastry and cut into strips.

Make a lattice shape over the mincemeat with the strips of pastry.

Bake in a hot oven until golden brown.

Serve straight from the oven sprinkled with icing sugar.

Delicious served with pouring cream, custard or brandy butter.

Brandy Butter

125g – 4oz Unsalted Butter
185g – 6oz Icing Sugar
4-8 Dessertspoons Brandy

Cream the butter until white.
Gradually add the sugar and the brandy.
Stand for a little time in a cold place to allow it to become really hard.

ALMOND SLICE

Ingredients

For the Pastry

500g – 1lb Golden Jewel Flour (or Plain Flour)
125g – 4oz Margarine or Butter
125g – 4oz White Flora
Cold Water to mix

For the Filling

3 Tablespoons Jam, Raspberry or Strawberry
185g – 6oz Ground Almonds
185g – 6oz Caster Sugar
2 Eggs – Beaten
½ Teaspoon Almond Extract
185g – 6oz Melted Butter
30g – 1oz Flaked Almonds

Lightly Greased Baking Tin – 11" / 28cm x 7" / 18cm
Oven 180°C / 350°F / Gas Mark 4
approximately 60 minutes

Put the flour, margarine and White Flora into the food processor and mix for a few seconds. Continue to mix adding the water a little at a time until a soft ball is formed.

Leave the pastry in the refrigerator for about ½ hour.

Roll out the pastry and line the tin.

Spread the jam over the pastry base.

Mix together all the filling ingredients, except the flaked almonds.

Pour the mixture over the jam and scatter the flaked almonds on top.

Bake for approximately 60 minutes until a golden colour.

Cool in the tin, before slicing into finger shapes.

Cakes and Sweets

MARMALADE BREAD PUDDING

Ingredients

1kg 500g – 3lb Bread (Crusts removed)

Juice of 3 Oranges

900ml – 1½ Pints Milk

750g – 1½ lb Mixed Fruit & Peel

375g – 12oz Dark Brown Sugar

280g – 9oz Soft Margarine or Butter

6 Teaspoons Mixed Spice

6 Tablespoons Marmalade

Extra Sugar for sprinkling
on top before serving.

Greaseproof Paper Lined Tin –
16" / 40cm x 10" / 25cm

Oven 180°C / 350°F / Gas Mark 4
1½ - 2 hours – cover part way through cooking

Soak the chopped bread in the milk for approximately one hour, and then add the rest of the ingredients. Mix well.

Turn the mixture into the greased and lined tin and bake slowly in the oven.

When cooked, divide into portions.

Best eaten hot, sprinkled with sugar, served with cream, custard or ice cream.

This recipe is always a good standby. The portions can be frozen and served at a later date.

This recipe is especially comforting on a cold winter's day.

Many years ago in my previous Teashop, a very elderly gentleman was so delighted at the prospect of bread pudding on the menu. He told us that his mother used to make it when he was a small boy. He said that on returning home from school she would hand them a piece and say 'ere, and don't go swimming'.

STICKY DATE CAKE
(pictured centre)

Ingredients

440g – 14oz Mixed Vine Fruits and Peel

250g – 8oz Chopped Pitted Dates

315g – 10oz Butter or Margarine

10 Fluid oz Water

405g – 14oz Tin Condensed Milk

155g – 5oz Plain Flour

155g – 5oz Wholemeal Flour

1 Pinch Salt

1 Level Teaspoon Bicarbonate of Soda

1 Tablespoon Chunky Marmalade

8 inch diameter deep cake tin fully lined

Oven 170°C / 2¹/₂ hours

Place the fruit/peel, margarine, water, dates and condensed milk in a saucepan and very gently bring to the boil, stirring all the time. Simmer, continuing to stir for 3 minutes.

Transfer the mixture to a large mixing bowl and cool for half an hour

Stir in the flour, salt, bicarbonate of soda and marmalade.

Transfer the mixture into the lined cake tin.

Cover the top with a double circle of greaseproof paper with a hole in the centre.

Bake for approximately 2¹/₂ hours in the centre of the oven.

As an extra treat, cover the whole cake with a Vanilla Butter icing.

Sylvia, a friend who worked for me for so many years in the Tea-Rooms always said this was her favourite cake. A treat at Christmas as an alternative to Christmas Cake.

PINEAPPLE FRUIT CAKE
(not illustrated)

Ingredients

185g – 6oz Soft Brown Sugar

375g – 12oz Mixed Fruit & Peel

125g – 4oz Halved Glace Cherries

125g – 4oz Butter

185g – 6oz Chopped Pineapple
(fresh or tinned)

185g – 6fl.oz Pineapple Juice

2 Eggs – Beaten

250g – 8oz Self-Raising Flour

Oven 160°C / 325°F / Gas Mark 3

Place all the ingredients except the eggs and flour into a saucepan. Mix well together. Gently bring to the boil, and simmer for 10 minutes.

Leave on the side to cool.

Add the beaten eggs and the self-raising flour and mix thoroughly.

Place the mixture in a fully lined 8" / 20cm cake tin and bake for 1¹/₂ - 2 hours.

A superbly moist fruit cake – could anything be nicer at 4 p.m. with a nice pot of tea.

GINGER CAKE

Ingredients

315g – 10oz Butter

375g – 12oz Black Treacle

250g – 8oz Soft Dark Brown Sugar

4 Eggs

1 Tablespoon Water

440gr – 14oz Self-Raising Flour

2 Teaspoons Grated Lemon Rind

4 Teaspoons Powdered Ginger

Crystallized Ginger for decoration

1 Square Tin 8" / 20cm x 8" / 20cm x 2" / 5cm deep
Oven 180°C / 350°F / Gas Mark 4

Put butter, sugar, treacle and water into a saucepan and heat gently until melted.

Sieve the dry ingredients together.

Pour the melted ingredients on to the dry mixture and beat thoroughly. Add the lemon rind and eggs.

Beat again and pour into the lined tin.

Cook in the centre of the oven for approximately 1 hour 15 minutes.

Ice the gingerbread and decorate with crystallized ginger.

Ginger Icing

4 Tablespoons Sifted Icing Sugar   1 Teaspoon Ground Ginger
30g – 1oz Butter   3 Teaspoons Golden Syrup

Place all the icing ingredients into a saucepan and cook over a low heat.
Stir continuously until boiling point is reached.

Before removing the cake from the tin, pour over the icing.
Decorate with preserved ginger and allow to cool.

Banana & Brazil Nut Loaf

Ingredients

250g – 8oz Butter or Margarine

250g – 8oz Granulated Sugar

250g – 8oz Self-Raising Flour

2 Level Teaspoons Baking Powder

4 Eggs

1½ Medium Bananas

125g – 4oz Brazil Nuts

Bread Tin 11½" / 29cm x 5" / 13cm x 3½" / 9cm deep

Oven 180°C / 350°F / Gas Mark 4

Put the butter, sugar, flour, baking powder and eggs into the food processor and mix thoroughly. Next, add the peeled bananas and Brazil nuts.

Continue mixing until you have a very soft consistency.

Pour the mixture into the greased and lined bread tin.

Bake in the oven for approximately 1¼-1½ hours, or until very firm to the touch. Cool in the tin before turning out.

Serve sliced, spread with butter.

This recipe is very versatile. It is equally delicious served as a plain cake. Iced with grated nuts on top, or as a hot pudding, sliced, warmed and served with pouring cream, custard or a hot sauce.

In order to vary the recipe, use hazel nuts or pecan nuts as an alternative to Brazil nuts.

If I am unable to purchase the special bread tin liners, I will always use 'Bakewell Paper' in preference to any other greaseproof paper.

ORANGE / APRICOT CAKE

Ingredients

250g – 8oz Butter
250g – 8oz Sugar (Granulated or Caster)
250g – 8oz Self-Raising Flour
1 Level Teaspoon Baking Powder
4 Eggs
Grated Rind of two Oranges
125g – 4oz Ready Soaked Dried Apricots

1 x 7" / 18cm diameter Cake Tin
3" / 8cm deep – greased and lined

Oven 180°C / 350°F / Gas Mark 4

Put the butter, sugar, flour, baking powder and eggs into a food processor and mix thoroughly, knocking down with a spatula from time to time.

Add the orange rind and apricots. Mix again until a nice soft consistency.

Pour the mixture into the prepared tin.

Cook for approximately 55 minutes until firm to the touch.

A moist cake delicious hot just as it comes out of the tin, or when cold. For that extra indulgence, fill the centre of the cake with apricot jam and fresh thick double cream or alternatively an orange butter cream.

Spread the top with icing and decorate with apricots.

COFFEE & WALNUT CAKE

Ingredients

250g – 8oz Margarine or Butter

250g – 8oz Sugar (Granulated or Caster)

250g – 8oz Self-Raising Flour

2 Level Teaspoons Baking Powder

4 Eggs

6 Heaped Teaspoons Instant Coffee (made into a thick paste using hot milk or water)

155g – 5oz Broken Walnuts

Two Cake Tins Greased and Lined – 9" / 23cm diameter x 1¹/₂" / 3.5cm deep

Oven 180°C / 350°F / Gas Mark 4

Put the margarine or butter, sugar, self-raising flour, baking powder and eggs into a food processor and mix until a soft mixture is achieved, knocking the mixture down twice during the mixing. Add the coffee paste and walnuts.

Continue mixing for a few seconds.

Divide the mixture between the two baking tins and bake in the oven for approximately 25-35 minutes, until the cake is firm to the touch.

Avoid opening the oven door during cooking if possible.

Pecan nuts are very successful in this recipe as an alternative to walnuts.

When the sponge is cold, fill the middle with a coffee butter cream, reserving a little to spread on top, which can then be sprinkled with crushed walnuts.

Coffee Butter Cream

250g – 8oz Butter

500g – 1lb Icing Sugar

2 Tablespoons Boiling Water

4 Tablespoons Instant Coffee

Combine all the ingredients to make a soft butter cream.

Coffee butter cream makes a nice alternative to icing the top of the cake.

Over the years, I would say this recipe has been the firm favourite cake with my gentlemen customers.

90

Apricot & Coconut Cake

Ingredients

250g – 8oz Margarine or Butter
250g – 8oz Sugar
(Granulated or Caster)

250g – 8oz Self-Raising Flour
2 Teaspoons Baking Powder
4 Large Eggs

185g – 6oz Pre-Soaked Dried Apricots
125g – 4oz Desiccated Coconut

Plus extra Coconut for Decoration
2 Tablespoons Apricot Jam

*Two Cake Tins greased and Lined –
9" / 23cm diameter x 1½" / 3.5cm deep*

*Oven 180°C / 350°F / Gas Mark 4
35-40 Minutes*

Put the margarine or butter, sugar, flour, baking powder and eggs into a food processor and mix until a soft consistency, knocking down from time to time.

Add the apricots and coconut and continue mixing for a further 10-15 seconds.

Divide the mixture into the two tins. Bake in the oven for approximately 35-40 minutes until firm to the touch.

When the sponge is cold, spread one-half with apricot jam and cover with fresh cream. Then place the top on. Spread the top with apricot jam and sprinkle with coconut.

This cake has always been a favourite in the Tea-Rooms.

Most of my customers seem to enjoy the flavour of apricots – always a popular choice.

LEMON POUND CAKE

Ingredients

250g – 8oz Butter

250g – 8oz Sugar

(Granulated or Caster)

250g – 8oz Self-Raising Flour

1 Teaspoon Baking Powder

Grated Rind of Two Lemons

4 Large Eggs

8" / 20cm Square Cake Tin
x 3" / 8cm deep greased and lined

Oven 180°C / 350°F / Gas Mark 4

Mix all the ingredients together in the food processor.

Knock down at least twice during mixing. Pour the mixture into the tin and bake in the oven for approximately 55 minutes.

When the cake is cold, cover the top with lemon icing.

Strictly speaking, this should be called a lemon 'half pound cake'. I believe the name derives from the fact that a pound of every ingredient is used in the recipe.

This recipe is wonderful with an afternoon cup of tea. My customers don't always wish to have cream in their cakes. A wonderful plain cake alternative. Lemon is always so refreshing.

Lemon Icing

15g - ½ oz Butter
2 Tablespoon Boiling Water
4 Teaspoons Lemon Juice
315g – 10oz Icing Sugar (sifted)

Melt the butter in the water, then stir in the lemon juice. Add the icing sugar a little at a time and beat until smooth. Spread evenly over the cake and allow to set.

FRUIT LOAVES

This recipe will make two large fruit loaves (or 4 x 1lb bread tin size). Use bread tins 11½" / 29cm x 5" / 13cm x 3½" / 9cm deep. It may seem extravagant but these will improve with keeping and are excellent if you wish to freeze them.

Ingredients

1k 500g – 3lb Mixed Dried Vine Fruit & Peel

500g – 1lb Granulated Sugar

32 fluid oz Cold Strong Tea (*I usually use Assam tea but equally successful with Earl Grey tea*)

1kg – 2lb Self-Raising Flour

4 Pinches Salt

4 Beaten Eggs

Oven 180°C / 350° / Gas Mark 4 approximately 2½-3 hours

Using a large mixing bowl put in the mixed fruit and peel, and sugar. Cover with the cold tea. Mix well, cover and leave overnight.

Next day, add the sifted flour, salt and eggs. Mix thoroughly. You will need to be strong; a little help may be required.

Divide the mixture into the two lined bread tins and place in the centre of the oven for approximately 2½-3 hours. You may need to cover the tops with Bakewell paper during cooking to prevent them from burning on top.

When cold, serve sliced with the option of lashings of butter. Try not to eat these loaves straightaway as they definitely improve with keeping.

95

LEMON AND SULTANA CAKE
(illustrated top and bottom)

Ingredients

250g – 8oz Butter or Margarine
250g – 8oz Granulated or Caster Sugar
250g – 8oz Self-Raising Flour
1 Level Teaspoon Baking Powder
4 Eggs
Grated Rind of two Lemons
125g – 4oz Sultanas

Two 9" / diameter Tins x 1¹/₂" / deep
Oven 180°C / 350°F / Gas Mark 4

Put the butter, sugar, flour, baking powder and eggs into the food processor and mix thoroughly. Knock down once with a spatula.

Add the grated rind of lemon and mix well. Knock down once again. Stop the machine and carefully fold in the sultanas with a spoon.

Divide the mixture carefully between the two greased and lined baking tins.

Bake in the oven for approximately 35 minutes. Try not to open the oven during cooking as this can result in the cake sinking in the middle.

When cold, spread one half with lemon curd and sandwich together with fresh double dairy cream.

Finally sprinkle sifted icing sugar on top.

As an alternative fill the cake with lemon butter cream and ice the top with lemon icing.

Lemon Butter Cream

185g – 6oz Butter, 185g – 6 Teaspoons Grated Lemon Rind
3 Dessertspoons Lemon Juice, 375g – 12oz Sieved Icing Sugar

Cream the butter and add the lemon rind. Gradually add the lemon juice and icing sugar alternatively to form a nice thick cream.

Lemon Icing

225g – 8oz Icing Sugar, 1¹/₂ Dessertspoons Lemon Juice

Blend the two ingredients together and spread over the top of the lemon cake.

FRESH CREAM ECLAIRS

Ingredients

Choux Pastry Ingredients

75g - 2½ oz Plain Flour
60g – 2oz Butter
¼ Teaspoon Salt
150ml - ¼ Pint Water
2 Eggs

Oven 200°C / 400°F / Gas Mark 5
25-30 Minutes

Chocolate Glacé Icing

250g – 8oz Icing Sugar (sifted)
Approx. 1½ Dessertspoons
Warm Water.

Gradually mix the icing sugar
and water together.

For chocolate flavouring add
1 good dessertspoon cocoa to
the icing and then beat in a
knob of melted butter about
the size of an acorn.

Sift the flour and salt into a basin and leave to one side.

Put the butter and water into a heavy-based pan and place over a low heat until the butter melts. Increase the heat and bring rapidly to the boil.

Remove the pan from the heat and pour in the sifted flour, stirring quickly until the flour has been absorbed into the liquid.

Return the pan to gentle heat, then cook for 2-3 minutes until the mixture is smooth and comes away from the side of the saucepan.

Cool the mixture for a few minutes, then beat in the eggs gradually. The pastry must be firm enough for piping, but not too stiff.

Pipe the mixture into finger shapes on well-greased and floured baking trays or put into greased and floured finger tins. Bake without covering for approximately 25-30 minutes until crisp.

Do not open the oven door whilst the pastry is cooking otherwise they may go flat.

When the pastry is cooked, split each puff open and leave in the oven for 30-60 seconds to dry the inside of the pastry.

When cold, fill each éclair with fresh thick dairy cream and cover the top with melted chocolate or chocolate glacé icing.

Top - Plain Shortbread Cir
covered with dairy cream and f
strawberies. As an alternative f
raspberries or any seasonal fr

FRESH CREAM MERINGUES

Delicious Served With
Seasonal Fresh Fruits

Ingredients

6 Egg Whites

375g – 12oz Caster Sugar

2 Teaspoons Cornflour

(optional)

1 Teaspoon Vinegar

1 Teaspoon Vanilla Extract

Oven 150° / 300° / Gas Mark 2
approximately one hour

Using an electric mixer, whisk the egg whites until very stiff.

Mix the caster sugar and cornflour together and add to the egg whites. Give the mixture a very quick stir.

Add the vinegar and give another quick stir.

Finally add the vanilla extract and give a final quick stir. Mix lightly with a tablespoon. It's as simple as that!

Line two baking sheets with Bakewell paper. Carefully put heaped spoonfuls of the mixture onto the baking sheets and bake in the oven for approximately one hour. Twist the trays round during cooking and swap from top to bottom shelves during cooking.

When cooled the meringues should be firm to the touch and lightly golden in colour.

When cold, sandwich the meringues together with fresh double cream and the fruit of your choice.

101

CHOCOLATE CHIP
SQUARES

Ingredients

185g – 6oz Butter

185g – 6oz Caster or Granulated Sugar

185g – 6oz Self-Raising Flour

1 Teaspoon Baking Powder

3 Large Eggs

3 Dessertspoons Cocoa Powder

2 Tablespoons Chocolate Chips

Melted Chocolate of your choice

Square Baking Tin greased and lined
7¹/₂" / 19cm x 7¹/₂" / 19cm

Oven 180°C / 350° / Gas Mark 4
approximately 50 minutes

Sieve the flour and baking powder together.

Cream together the butter and sugar in a large mixing bowl.

Add the sieved flour and eggs alternately and continue to mix thoroughly.

Carefully blend in the cocoa powder and lastly mix in the chocolate chips.

Pour the mixture into the lined tin and bake in the oven for approximately 50 minutes or until firm to the touch.

Allow to cool before pouring the melted chocolate over the top, and dividing into squares.

Place small Easter eggs on top for that extra Easter treat.

Alternatively, this recipe could be divided into two lined sponge tins, cooked for 35 minutes and when cold, sandwiched together with fresh cream or chocolate butter cream.

VICTORIA SPONGE CAKE

Ingredients

315g – 10oz Margarine or Butter

315g – 10oz Sugar
(Granulated or Caster)

315g – 10oz Self-Raising Flour

2 Teaspoons Baking Powder

5 Large Eggs

1 Teaspoon Vanilla Essence

*Two Cake Tins Greased and Lined –
9" / 23cm diameter x 1¹/₂" / 3.5cm deep*

Oven 180°C /350°F / Gas Mark 4

For a smaller cake, just simply reduce the ingredients.

Put all the ingredients into a food processor and mix together, knocking down from time to time.

When the mixture is nice and liquid, divide into the two tins. Bake in the oven for approximately 30-35 minutes, until firm to the touch. Avoid opening the oven door whilst the sponge is cooking as this can cause the sponge to sink in the middle.

When cold, fill the middle with jam and thick fresh cream. Sprinkle icing sugar on top.

Always a favourite with my customers. For whatever reason some people seem afraid of making sponge cakes, but really, they are very quick and easy.

BASIC SPONGE CAKE –
Using an Electric Mixer

Ingredients

6oz Butter or Margarine
at room temperature
6oz Sugar (Granulated or Caster)
6oz Self-Raising Flour
1 Teaspoon Baking Powder
3 Large Eggs
1 Teaspoon Vanilla Essence
2 Heaped Tablespoons Jam

2 x 7" Sandwich Tins
Oven 180°C / 350° F / Gas Mark 4
25-30 Minutes

Grease and line two 7" (18cm) Sandwich Tins.

Pre-heat the oven to moderately hot.

Place the butter and sugar in the mixing bowl. Combine the ingredients together on speed 2 and then increase to a high speed and mix until light and fluffy.

Add the eggs on maximum speed a little at a time, beating thoroughly after each addition.

Reduce to minimum speed and add the flour. Mix until all the flour has been incorporated.

Turn into two greased 7" tins and bake at 180°C for 25-30 minutes until firm to the touch.

Allow to stand in the tin for a few minutes before turning them out. Remove the lining paper and cool on a wire tray. When cold, sandwich together with the jam or jam and thick dairy cream. Sprinkle the top with sugar.

If you wish to flavour the sponge cakes, try the following suggestions:

You will need to **omit** the vanilla essence from the list of ingredients.

Chocolate Flavour: Blend two tablespoons of cocoa with 4 Tablespoons boiling water. Allow the paste to cool before adding to the mixture. Sandwich together with thick dairy cream or chocolate butter cream.

Coffee: 1½ Tablespoons coffee essence or strong black coffee. Sandwich together with coffee flavoured butter cream.

Orange: Grated rind of two oranges. Sandwich together with orange flavoured butter cream.

Lemon: Grated rind of two lemons. Sandwich together with lemon curd and fresh thick dairy cream.

BASIC SPONGE CAKE RECIPE –

Hand Method

Most of the cakes I make for the tea-rooms are very large. All the ingredients can naturally be reduced to produce a smaller cake. The following recipe will make an average size sponge cake:

Ingredients

6oz Butter or Margarine at room temperature

6oz Sugar *(Granulated or Caster)*

6oz Self-Raising Flour

1 Teaspoon Baking Powder

3 Large Eggs

1 Teaspoon Vanilla Essence

2 Heaped Tablespoons Jam

Caster Sugar for sprinkling

2 x 7" / 18cm Round Cake Tins

Oven 180°C / 350° F / Gas Mark 4
25-30 Minutes

Grease and line two 7" cake tins.
Pre-heat the oven 180°C.

In a large mixing bowl, cream the butter and sugar until pale and fluffy, then beat in the eggs, a little at a time.

Fold in the sifted flour and baking powder as lightly as possible.

Pour the mixture evenly into the tins, level and bake for approximately 25-30 minutes until firm to the touch.

Allow to stand in the tin for a few minutes, then turn out, remove the lining paper and cool on a wire tray.

When cold, sandwich the sponges together with the jam of your choice and sprinkle the top with sugar.

For that extra treat, sandwich the cake together with jam and thick dairy cream.

Margaret's Recipes *From Her Tea Rooms*

Margaret's Recipes *From Her Tea Rooms*

SMALL BUNS AND BUTTERFLY CAKES

Ingredients

185g – 6oz Butter

185g – 6oz Caster or
Granulated Sugar

185g – 6oz Self-Raising Flour

1 Teaspoon Baking Powder

3 Eggs – Beaten

Oven 190° / 375° / Gas 4

Sieve together the Self-Raising flour and baking powder.

Cream the butter and sugar together until light and fluffy.

Beat the eggs into the creamed mixture alternately with the flour.

Line patty tins with small cake cases.

Spoon the mixture into the cases, dividing equally.

Bake in the pre-heated oven for 7-10 minutes.

Cool on a wire rack.

When the cakes are completely cold decorate with coloured glacé icing or melted chocolate on top.

Alternatively cut out a circle of sponge from the top of each cake and cut the circle in half. Put butter cream in the centre of the cake and replace the two halves to resemble a butterfly shape.

Glacé Icing

185g – 6oz Icing Sugar (sifted)
1-2 Tablespoons Warm Water or other Liquid
such as Lemon or Orange Juice.
Flavouring of your choice.

Sift the icing sugar into a bowl and add the water a little at a time. Mix until the icing is smooth and thick enough to coat the back of a spoon.

Add any flavouring of your choice.

Butter Cream

125g – 4oz Butter – softened but not oily
250g – 8oz Icing Sugar (sifted)
1 Tablespoon Milk
Flavouring of your choice

Beat the butter until pale.
Gradually beat in the icing sugar until the mixture is fluffy. Add the milk, work in a little flavouring of your choice. As an alternative to plain cakes, add coconut, currants, cherries or chocolate chips.

DUNDEE CAKE

Ingredients

250g – 8oz Butter, softened
1 Teaspoon Rum Essence
220g – 7oz Caster Sugar
4 Eggs – Lightly Beaten
250g – 8oz Self-Raising Flour
1 Teaspoon Baking Powder
3 Tablespoons Cornflour
500g – 1lb Mixed Fruit
125g – 4oz Mixed Peel
125g – 4oz Slivered Almonds
125g – 4oz Glacé Cherries, Halved
3 Teaspoons Finely Grated Orange Rind
2 Tablespoons Orange Juice
60g – 2oz Blanched Almonds

Oven 150°C / 300°F / Gas Mark 2
2½-3 hours

Place butter and rum essence in a bowl and beat until light and fluffy. Gradually add the sugar, beating well after each addition until the mixture is creamy.

Add the eggs one at a time, beating well after each addition.

Sift together flour, baking powder and cornflour and fold into the butter mixture.

Stir in the mixed fruit, mixed peel, slivered almonds, cherries, orange rind and orange juice. Spoon the mixture into a greased and lined deep 8-inch / 20cm cake tin.

Decorate the top of the cake with blanched almonds arranged in circles and bake for 2½ - 3 hours or until cooked when tested with a skewer.

Cool in the tin before turning out.

SIMNEL CAKE

Ingredients

185g – 6oz Butter
185g – 6oz Sugar
250g – 8oz Plain Flour
1½ Level Teaspoons Baking Powder
3 Eggs
500g – 1lb Mixed Dried Fruit
125g – 4oz Chopped Almonds
60g – 2oz Glacé Cherries, 2oz Peel
2 Tablespoons Milk, 1 Teaspoon Spice

8" Round Cake Tin
Oven 180°C / 350°F / Gas Mark 3
Bake 2 - 2¼ hours in the centre of the oven

Cream the butter and sugar together until soft. Add the beaten egg. Sieve the dry ingredients together. Mix the almonds, cherries, fruit and peel together. Stir in the flour and enough milk to make a dropping consistency, and lastly put in the fruit.

Make home-made marzipan. Roll out and cut into two circles, one slightly smaller than the diameter of the cake.

Put half the cake mixture into the lined cake tin and cover with the smaller round marzipan. Add the rest of the cake mixture and bake in the oven as directed.

When baked and cool, brush the top of the cake with egg white or sieved apricot jam. Cover with the second round of marzipan. Decorate the edges. Brush with egg white and brown under a low grill. For an Easter cake decorate with eleven tiny Easter eggs.

Margaret's Recipes From Her Tea Rooms

Margaret's Recipes *From Her Tea Rooms*

RICH FRUIT CAKE

(Suitable for a Christmas Cake)

Ingredients

315g – 10oz Butter

155g – 5oz Caster Sugar

155g – 5oz Soft Brown Sugar

375g – 12oz Plain Flour

Pinch Salt

5 Eggs

½ Teaspoon Ground Nutmeg

1 Teaspoon Cinnamon

250g – 8oz Currants

250g – 8oz Sultanas

250g – 8oz Seedless Raisins

185g – 6oz Glacé Cherries

125g – 4oz Candied Peel

Grated Rind and Juice of 1 Orange or Lemon

60g – 2oz Chopped Walnuts

60g – 2oz Chopped Almonds

2 Tablespoons Brandy or Sherry

*8" / 20cm Round Cake Tin –
greased and lined with greaseproof paper.
Double layer of brown paper tied
around the outside of the tin.*

*Oven 150°C / 300°F / Gas Mark 2 for 2 hours.
Reduce heat for further 2 hours.*

Cream together the butter and sugars. Beat the eggs and gradually add to the butter and sugars, together with the flour and spices.

Fold in the rest of the flour, salt, fruit, peel, glacé cherries, nuts, orange or lemon, brandy or sherry.

When evenly mixed, turn into a lined 8" diameter cake tin and make a slight hollow in the centre.

Bake at 150°C for approximately 2 hours, then reduce the heat for 2 hours. Cover with greaseproof paper if browning too quickly on top.

If making the cake for Christmas, make approximately three weeks beforehand. Decorate with marzipan and icing about one week before Christmas.

MARZIPAN

Ingredients

250g – 8oz Ground Almonds
125g – 4oz Caster Sugar
125g – 4oz Icing Sugar (Sieved)
1 Teaspoon Lemon Juice
1½ Teaspoons Almond Extract
1 Egg White

Oven 160°C / 325°F / Gas Mark 3

Place the ground almonds and sugars into a bowl.

Make a well in the centre and add the lemon juice, almond extract and egg white.

Mix to a soft dough.

Sprinkle a working surface with icing sugar and knead until smooth. Wrap in cling film until ready to use.

ROYAL ICING

Ingredients

2 Egg Whites
500g – 1lb Icing Sugar
½ Tablespoon Lemon Juice
1 Teaspoon Glycerine (optional)

Oven 160°C / 325°F / Gas Mark 3

Whisk the egg whites in a large bowl until frothy.

Sieve and stir in the icing sugar a little at a time and mix thoroughly.

When half the sugar has been added, beat in the lemon juice and continue to add more sugar, mixing well after each addition.

If possible, leave the icing to rest for 24 hours to allow air bubbles to rise to the surface. Work it through again before using.

CARROT & WALNUT CAKE

Ingredients

250g – 8oz Grated Carrot
250g – 8oz Chopped Walnuts
250g – 8oz Margarine or Butter
250g – 8oz Soft Brown Sugar
185g – 6oz Wholemeal Flour
3 Eggs

1½ Teaspoons Bicarbonate of Soda
1½ Teaspoons Baking Powder
1½ Teaspoons Ground Cinnamon
½ Teaspoon Salt
1 Teaspoon Vanilla Extract

7" / 18cm Round Cake Tin
x 3" / 8cm deep – greased and lined

Oven 180°C / 350°F / Gas Mark 4

In a mixer, cream together the margarine and sugar.

Gradually add the flour and eggs alternately.

Next, add the bicarbonate of soda, baking powder, cinnamon, salt and vanilla extract.

Lastly add the grated carrot and walnuts. Mix well.

Pour into a lined 7" cake tin and cook in the centre of the oven for approximately 1-1½ hours, until firm to the touch.

Leave the cake in the tin until cold before turning out of the tin.

Cover the top of the cake with a cream cheese frosting, a rum icing or an orange icing.

Toppings for Carrot Cake

CREAM CHEESE FROSTING

Ingredients

125g – 4oz Cream Cheese
60g – 2oz Butter or Margarine
1 Level Teaspoon Vanilla Extract
315g – 10oz Icing Sugar

Place cream cheese and butter (room temperature) in a bowl. Beat until creamy and gradually add the icing sugar, and vanilla extract. Spread on to the top of the cake and decorate with broken walnuts.

RUM ICING

Ingredients

220g – 7oz Icing Sugar
2 Tablespoons Rum
1 Tablespoon Lemon Juice

Combine all the ingredients and spread over the cake. Decorate with chopped walnuts.

ORANGE ICING

Ingredients

45g - 1½ oz Butter or Margarine
155g – 5oz Soft Pale Brown Sugar
Grated Rind of 1 Orange
30g – 1oz Chopped Walnuts

Beat the butter until soft. Mix in the sugar and orange rind. Spread over the cake and sprinkle with chopped walnuts.

QUICK & EASY
FRUIT CAKE

Ingredients

185g – 6oz Demerara Sugar

440g – 14oz Mixed Vine Fruits & Peel

300ml / ½ Pint Water

90g – 3oz Glacé Cherries

125g – 4oz Butter

Pinch Salt

1 Beaten Egg

315g – 10oz Self-Raising Flour

60g – 2oz Blanched Almonds or
1oz Flaked Almonds

30g – 1oz Glacé Cherries

7" / 18cm diameter Cake Tin 3" / 8cm deep
Oven 180°C / 350°F / Gas Mark 4

Put the sugar in a saucepan with the fruit and peel, water, cherries, butter and salt.

Bring to the boil carefully and simmer for 20 minutes.

Allow to cool.

Add the egg to the cooled mixture. Then add the flour and mix thoroughly.

Turn into the prepared tin and smooth the top.

Arrange the almonds and cherries on top.

Bake in the oven for 1½ - 2 hours until risen and golden brown.

MINCE PIES

Ingredients

500g – 1lb Golden Jewel Flour (or Plain Flour)

125g – 4oz Margarine or Butter

125g – 4oz White Flora

Approx. 3 Tablespoons Cold Water

Mincemeat - preferably home-made

*Combine all the ingredients
in the food processor.*

*Knead lightly, wrap and chill for
approximately half hour.*

*Pre-heat the oven to 180°C / 350°F /
Gas Mark 4*

Roll out the pastry on a floured surface and cut 12 three-inch rounds with a pastry cutter.

Put into greased tartlet cases. Spoon the mincemeat into the cases. Use the remaining pastry to roll out and cut lids to the decorative shape of your choice.

For the citrus pastry, add the grated rind of one orange or lemon to the other pastry ingredients.

For the shortcrust topping, cream together the following ingredients:

185g – 6oz Self-Raising Flour

185g – 6oz Margarine or Butter

60g – 2oz Sugar

1 Tablespoon Rum or Brandy

Spread on top of the mincemeat. Sprinkle with sugar and decorate with a half-glacé cherry on top.

The Golden Jewel flour is a very tasty pastry flour; it is blended with maize flour which gives a nice golden finish.

If you are not familiar with this flour, 1 purchase it from Letheringsett Water Mill. 'Mike the Miller' delivers the flours to the Tea-Rooms on a weekly basis, thus ensuring the freshness.

BRANDY SNAPS

Ingredients

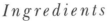

125g – 4oz Butter

315g – 10oz Caster Sugar

2 Rounded Tablespoons
Golden Syrup

90g – 3oz Plain Flour

1 Teaspoon Ground Ginger

*Baking Trays lined with
Bakewell paper*

*Oven 190°C / 375°F /
Gas Mark 4*

Cream together the butter and sugar in an electric mixer. Then beat in the golden syrup. Add the sifted flour and ginger and mix to a soft dough.

(Alternatively place all the ingredients in a food processor and process until a rough dough is formed.)

Knead the dough until smooth.

Cover and chill for 30 minutes.

Put teaspoons of the mixture on to prepared Bakewell paper, five inches apart.

Bake for 8-10 minutes until they are rich brown in colour and well spread on the paper.

Remove from the oven and leave to cool for a moment, until they can be easily lifted.

While still warm, wrap each one around a wooden spoon handle. You will need to work quickly.

Allow them to become firm before lifting on to a wire rack.

Serve filled with fresh cream or whipped cream mixed with two tablespoons of Brandy.

Delicious also, coated in melted chocolate.

WYN'S CHRISTMAS PUDDING

Ingredients

250g – 8oz Soft Margarine
500g – 1lb Raisins
500g – 1lb Sultanas
125g – 4oz Candied Peel
185g – 6oz Soft Dark Brown Sugar
185g – 6oz Self-Raising Flour
30g – 1oz Sweet Almonds (Chopped)
Grated Rind and Juice of 1 Lemon
3 Large Eggs
250g – 8oz Breadcrumbs
Half a nutmeg - Grated
4-5 Tablespoons Rum
Pinch Salt
Milk to mix

Oven 160°C / 325°F / Gas Mark 3

Clean the dried fruit thoroughly.

Put all the dry ingredients into a large bowl, followed by the blanched almonds, the beaten eggs, grated rind and juice of lemon.

Mix thoroughly.

Add the alcohol and sufficient milk, to a dropping consistency. Stir well.

Leave for between 24-48 hours before mixing thoroughly again.

Transfer the mixture to the basins. This quantity should be sufficient for 4 x 1lb Puddings.

Place greaseproof paper over the puddings and cover with a tied cloth.

Steam for 6-8 hours.

The puddings should keep for up to one year if kept in a cool dry place.

When ready to eat, re-heat for 2-4 hours.

APPLE / SULTANA CAKE

Ingredients

250g – 8oz Sultanas

250g – 8oz Cooking Apples
(Peeled, Cored and Chopped)

150ml / ¼ Pint Milk

185g – 6oz Soft Brown Sugar

375g – 12oz Self-Raising Flour

2 Teaspoons Mixed Spice

Grated Rind of one Lemon

185g – 6oz Butter Melted

1 Beaten Egg

60g – 2oz Demerara Sugar

1 x 7" / 18cm Cake Tin
3" / 8cm deep – greased and lined
Oven 180° / 350°F / Gas Mark 4

Mix the sultanas, apples and milk and leave to one side.

Mix together the brown sugar, flour, spice and lemon rind. Gradually blend in the butter and egg.

Mix in the fruit mixture and beat well.

Turn into the prepared tin.

Sprinkle the Demerara sugar on top.

Bake in the pre-heated oven for approximately 1½ hours, until firm to the touch.

To enjoy this cake at its best keep for a day or two.

Margaret's Recipes *From Her Tea Rooms*